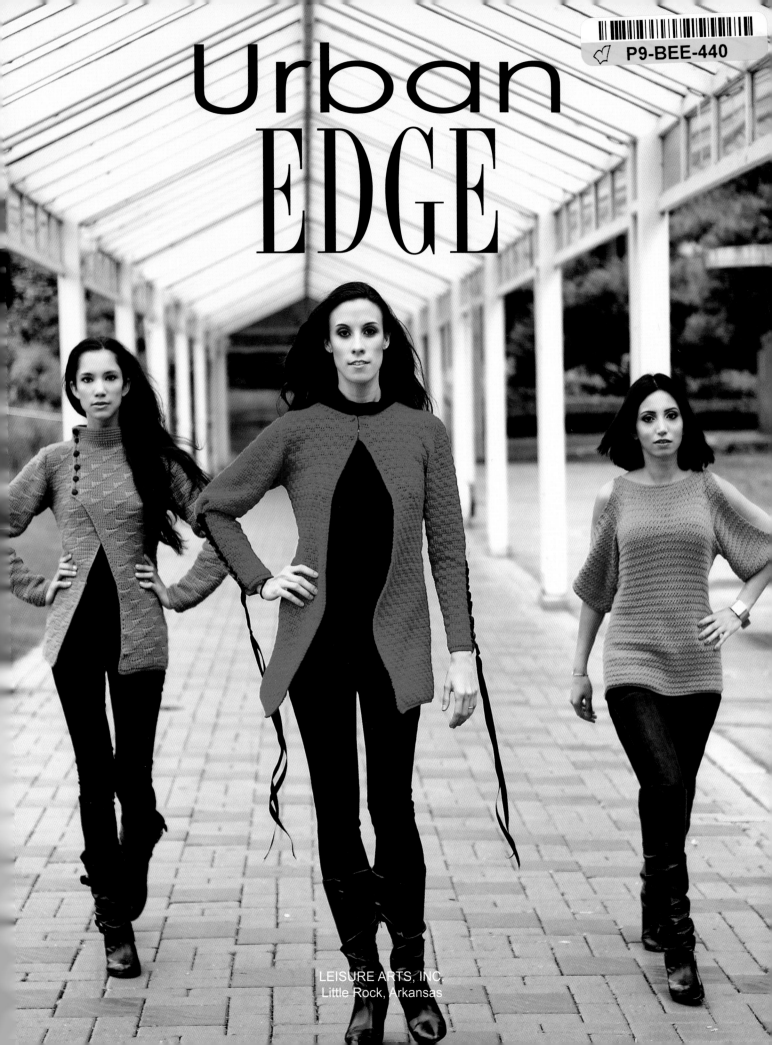

Urban
EDGE

P9-BEE-440

LEISURE ARTS, INC.
Little Rock, Arkansas

SHIBAGUYZ DESIGNZ STAFF
Graphic Designer: Jason Mullett-Bowlsby
Photographer: Jason Mullett-Bowlsby for Shibaguyz Designz
Makeup: Chelsey Duff
Tech Editor: KJ Hay
Photo Assistant: Kathy Cadigan
Models: Andrea Pons, Michelle Green, Jayme Johnson,
  Lindsi Dec, Negar Niromand Hosseini

LEISURE ARTS STAFF
EDITORIAL
Vice President and Editor-in-Chief: Susan White Sullivan
Knit and Crochet Publications Director: Lindsay White Glenn
Special Projects Director: Susan Frantz Wiles
Senior Prepress Director: Mark Hawkins
Art Publications Director: Rhonda Shelby
Editorial Writer: Susan McManus Johnson
Art Category Manager: Lora Puls
Imaging Technician: Stephanie Johnson
Prepress Technician: Janie Marie Wright
Publishing Systems Administrator: Becky Riddle
Mac Information Technology Specialist: Robert Young

BUSINESS
President and Chief Executive Officer: Rick Barton
Vice President of Sales: Mike Behar
Director of Finance and Administration: Laticia Mull Dittrich
Director of Corporate Planning: Anne Martin
National Sales Director: Martha Adams
Creative Services: Chaska Lucas
Information Technology Director: Hermine Linz
Controller: Francis Caple
Vice President, Operations: Jim Dittrich
Retail Customer Service Manager: Stan Raynor
Print Production Manager: Fred F. Pruss

Copyright © 2012 by Leisure Arts, Inc., 5701 Ranch Drive, Little
Rock, Arkansas 72223-9633. All rights reserved. This publication
is protected under federal copyright laws. Reproduction of
this publication or any other Leisure Arts publication, including
publications which are out of print, is prohibited unless specifically
authorized. This includes, but is not limited to, any form of
reproduction or distribution on or through the Internet, including
posting, scanning or e-mail transmission. We have made every
effort to ensure that these instructions are accurate and complete.
We cannot, however, be responsible for human error, typographical
mistakes, or variations in individual work. Made in China.

Library of Congress Control Number: 2011941245

ISBN-13: 9781609006617

Contents

Introduction

Hey there Stitchers!

Urban Edge is the culmination of many months of thought, planning and hard work… and now you have it in your hands. WOOHOO!!

Even though I grew up on a farm and honor that heritage daily, my life under the bright lights of the city is what has inspired me to create this collection of designs for you. The visual excitement of the urban lifestyle, the stunning architecture of the city and the versatility and adaptability of the people gave me the inspiration for the designs on these pages and I am beyond thrilled that you will be stitching these patterns for yourself.

Early in my design career, I had this wonderful realization that, as a designer of hand-stitched garments, I was able to create my own unique fabrics that specifically complimented my original designs. This lightning bolt of revelation has guided me to be fearless when it comes to creating designs and has given me a unique perspective as a crochet designer. The possibilities are endless!

My vision for this book is to share some of these exciting design possibilities with you while also providing you, the stitcher, with some essential tools to give you the greatest chance for success. These tools are generously distributed throughout this book in the form of written instructions, pattern notes, in-line pattern notes, Craft Yarn Council of America guidelines for helping you choose yarns, stitch guides and illustrations.

As an added feature, we have also included some of my own personal tutorials for foundations and finishing techniques. These tutorials include step-by-step instructions, illustrations and photos for starting and finishing your projects just like some of the techniques I teach in my "Fab Foundations and Finishing" classes.

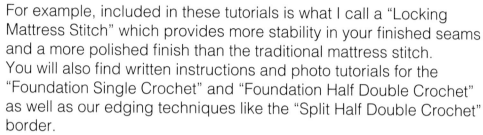

For example, included in these tutorials is what I call a "Locking Mattress Stitch" which provides more stability in your finished seams and a more polished finish than the traditional mattress stitch. You will also find written instructions and photo tutorials for the "Foundation Single Crochet" and "Foundation Half Double Crochet" as well as our edging techniques like the "Split Half Double Crochet" border.

In the end, I have worked to create a book that includes exciting and versatile designs that are interesting to make and important instructional materials that help you enjoy the process of stitching those designs for yourself. I mean c'mon, what is the point of making a garment that doesn't energize you?

One more thing; even if a pattern is listed at a skill level above your current knowledge, work on the swatch as a way to learn the skills necessary to create the garments. You soon will have the experience needed to make that garment you want.

I am proud to share these patterns with you and I hope you find the vibrancy, versatility and excitement of these designs as exciting to stitch as they were for me to create.

Stitch On!
Shannon Mullett-Bowlsby

Dublin

I have always loved the striking look of the cables in Aran sweaters and I also love the way a great sweater dress looks fantastic on such a wide range of body types. I combined classic Aran cables with a sweater dress silhouette to create luxury with a funky twist. You will feel fantastic in this piece whether you are shopping downtown or taking a casual stroll along the waterfront on a cool day.

SKILL LEVEL: ◖■■■▶ EXPERIENCED

SIZE: Small {Medium, Large, 1X, 2X, 3X}

FINISHED MEASUREMENTS:
To Fit Bust: 36 {40, 44, 48, 52, 56}" / 91.5 {101.5, 112, 122, 132, 142} cm
Length: 30¹/₂ {30¹/₂, 31, 31, 31¹/₂, 31¹/₂}" / 77.5 {77.5, 78.5, 78.5, 80, 80} cm not including lower cable border

SIZE NOTE:
Instructions are written for Small size with changes for larger sizes in braces { }. Instructions will be easier to read if you circle all the numbers pertaining to your size. If only one number is given it pertains to all sizes.

MATERIALS
Medium Weight Yarn
[2.5 ounces, 138 yards (70.8 grams, 127 meters) per ball]: 18 {20, 22, 24, 27, 29} balls
Shown In: Naturally Caron.com JOY (70% Acrylic/30% Rayon from bamboo; 2.5oz/70.8g, 138yds/127m): Color #0003 Sunset
Crochet Hook: Size F-5 (3.75 mm) **or** size needed for Gauge
Stitch Markers
Yarn Needle

BLOCKED GAUGE:
In Cable Pattern (lower section), 14 sts = 3¹/₄" (8.5 cm) and 16 rows = 4" (10 cm);
In main body pattern, 25 sts = 6" (15 cm) and 16 rows = 5" (12.5 cm);
In Sleeve Cable Pattern, 21 sts = 5" (12.5 cm) and 25 rows = 8" (20.5 cm).
Fsc 28, turn.

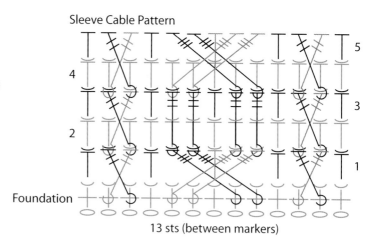

Sleeve Cable Pattern

13 sts (between markers)

Lower Cable Pattern

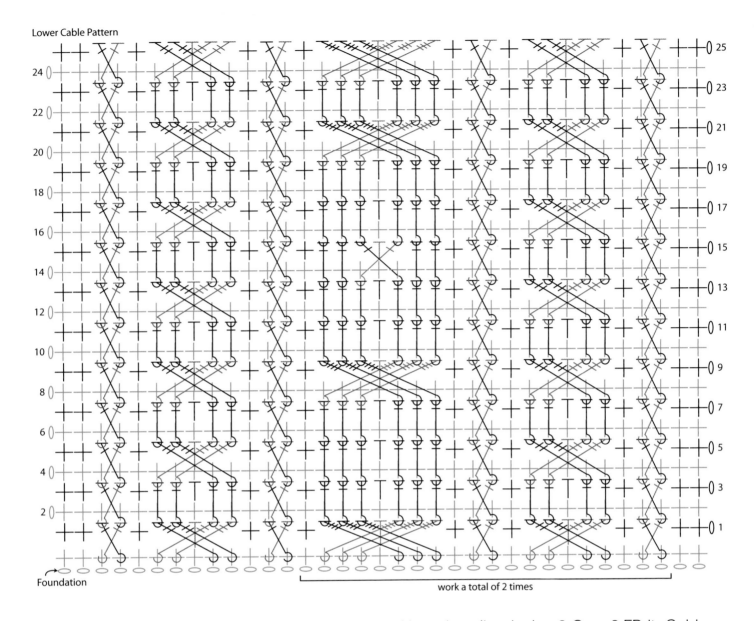

Foundation

work a total of 2 times

GAUGE SWATCH #1: Cable pattern – Block to 6 ½ x 6" (16.5 x 15 cm)

Row 1 (RS): Ch 1, sc in first 3 sts, sk next st, FPdc around next st, FPdc around skipped st (beginning FPdc-Cross-St made), sc in next st; sk next 3 sts, FPtr around each of next 2 sts, working behind FPtr just made, hdc in 3rd skipped st, working in front of FPtr just made, FPtr around each of first 2 skipped sts (beginning 2-Over-2 FPtr-Cable made); sc in next st, work beginning FPdc-Cross-St, sc in next st; sk next 4 sts, FPdtr around each of next 3 sts, working behind FPdtr just made, hdc in 4th skipped st, working in front of FPdtr just made, FPdtr around each of first 3

skipped sts (beginning 3-Over-3 FPdtr-Cable made);, sc in next st, work beginning FPdc-Cross-St, sc in last 3 sts, turn.

Row 2: Ch 1, sc in each st across, turn.

Row 3: Ch 1, sc in first 3 sts, FPdc-Cross-St, sc in next st, FPdc around each of next 2 sts 2 rows below, hdc in next st, FPdc around each of next 2 sts 2 rows below, sc in next st, FPdc-Cross-St, sc in next st, FPdc around each of next 3 sts 2 rows below, hdc in next st, FPdc around each of next 3 sts 2 rows below, sc in next st, FPdc-Cross-St, sc in last 3 sts, turn.

8 **www.leisurearts.com**

Row 4: Ch 1, sc in each st across, turn.

Row 5: Ch 1, sc in first 3 sts, FPdc-Cross-St, sc in next st, work 2-Over-2 FPtr-Cable over next 5 sts, sc in next st, FPdc-Cross-St, sc in next st, FPdc around each of next 3 sts 2 rows below, hdc in next st, FPdc around each of next 3 sts 2 rows below, sc in next st, FPdc-Cross-St, sc in last 3 sts, turn.

Rows 6–8: Repeat Rows 2–4.

Row 9: Ch 1, sc in first 2 sts, [FPdc-Cross-St, sc in next st, work 2-Over-2 FPtr-Cable over next 5 sts, sc in next st, FPdc-Cross-St, sc in next st, work 3-Over-3 FPdtr-Cable over next 7 sts, sc in next st] 2 times, FPdc-Cross-St, sc in next st, work 2-Over-2 FPtr-Cable over next 5 sts, sc in next sc, FPdc-Cross-St, sc in last 2 sts, turn.

Rows 10–14: Repeat Rows 2–6.

Row 15: Ch 1, sc in first 3 sts, FPdc-Cross-St, sc in next st, FPdc around each of next 2 sts 2 rows below, hdc in next st, FPdc around each of next 2 sts 2 rows below, sc in next st, FPdc-Cross-St, sc in next st, FPdc around each of next 2 sts 2 rows below, 1-over-1 FPdc-Cable over next 3 sts, FPdc around next 2 sts 2 rows below, sc in next st, FPdc-Cross-St, sc in last 3 sts, turn.

Rows 16–24: Repeat Rows 4–12.
Fasten off.

GAUGE SWATCH #2: Main body pattern – Block to 6 x 5" (15 x 12.5 cm)
Fhdc 25, turn.

Rows 1–15: Ch 1, sc in first st; sc FLO in each st across to last st; sc in last st, turn.
Fasten off

STITCH GUIDE

1-Over-1 FPdc-Cable (worked over 3 sts): Sk next 2 sts, FPdc around next st 2 rows below; working behind FPdc just made, hdc in 2nd skipped st, working in front of FPdc just made, FPdc around first skipped st 2 rows below.

2-Over-2 FPtr-Cable (worked over 5 sts): Sk next 3 sts, FPtr around each of next 2 sts 2 rows below; working behind FPtr just made, hdc in 3rd skipped st; working in front of FPtr just made, FPtr around each of first 2 skipped sts 2 rows below.

2-Over-2 FPdtr-Cable (worked over 5 sts): Sk next 3 sts, FPdtr around each of next 2 sts 2 rows below; working behind FPdtr just made, hdc in 3rd skipped st; working in front of FPdtr just made, FPdtr around each of first 2 skipped sts 2 rows below.

3-Over-3 FPdtr-Cable (worked over 7 sts): Sk next 4 sts, FPdtr around each of next 3 sts 2 rows below; working behind FPdtr just made, hdc in 4th skipped st; working in front of FPdtr just made, FPdtr around each of first 3 skipped sts 2 rows below.

FPdc-Cross-St: Sk next st, FPdc around next st 2 rows below; working in front of FPdc just made, FPdc around skipped st 2 rows below.

FPtr-Cross-St: Sk next st, FPtr around next st 2 rows below; working in front of FPtr just made, FPtr around skipped st 2 rows below.

Foundation Single Crochet (Fsc): Ch 2, insert hook in 2nd ch from hook, yo and draw up a loop, yo and draw through 1 loop (first "chain" made), yo and draw through 2 loops on hook (first sc made), ✳ insert hook under 2 loops of the "chain" just made, yo and draw up a loop, yo and draw through 1 loop ("chain" made), yo and draw through 2 loops on hook (sc made); repeat from ✳ for desired number of foundation stitches. *(See page 94)*

Foundation Half Double Crochet (Fhdc):
Ch 2, yo, insert hook in 2nd ch from hook, yo and draw up a loop, yo and draw through 1 loop (first "chain" made), yo and draw through 3 loops on hook (first hdc made), ✳ yo, insert hook under 2 loops of the "chain" just made, yo and draw up a loop, yo and draw through 1 loop ("chain" made), yo and draw through 3 loops on hook (hdc made); repeat from ✳ for desired number of foundation stitches. **(See page 94)**

Front-Post Double Crochet (FPdc): Yo, insert hook from front to back and then to front again around post of stitch, yo and draw up loop, [yo and draw through 2 loops on hook] twice. **(See Fig. 2, page 93)**

Front-Post Treble Crochet (FPtr): [Yo] twice, insert hook from front to back and then to front again around post of stitch, yo and draw up a loop, [yo and draw through 2 loops on hook] 3 times.

Front-Post Double Treble Crochet (FPdtr): [Yo] 3 times, insert hook from front to back and then to front again around post of stitch, yo and draw up a loop, [yo and draw through 2 loops on hook] 4 times.

Notes:
1. Tunic is made in six sections: a lower cable section, front, back, two sleeves, and a cowl neck.
2. The lower cable section is worked sideways and sewn to lower edge of tunic during finishing.
3. The sleeves have saddle shoulders. Each sleeve is worked from cuff up to neckline. A cable pattern is worked up the center of each sleeve and across the saddle shoulder.
4. After the other five sections are assembled, the cowl neck is worked in rounds around the neck edge.
5. Post stitches (FPdc, FPtr and FPdtr) are always worked around the post of stitches two rows below the working row (except when working Row 1).

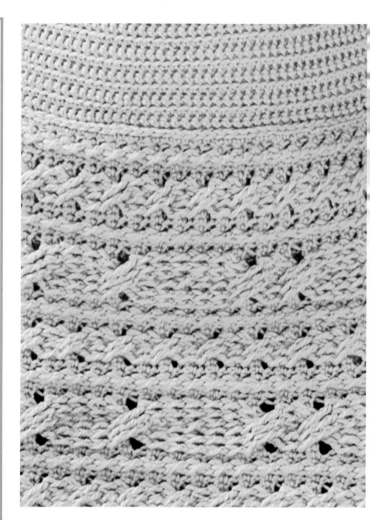

Dublin Cables Dress ⚐

LOWER CABLE SECTION

Fsc 55, turn.

Row 1 (RS): Ch 1, sc in first 2 sts, [sk next st, FPdc around next st, FPdc around skipped st (beginning FPdc-Cross-St made), sc in next st; sk next 3 sts, FPtr around each of next 2 sts, working behind FPtr just made, hdc in 3rd skipped st, working in front of FPtr just made, FPtr around each of first 2 skipped sts (beginning 2-Over-2 FPtr-Cable made); sc in next st, work beginning FPdc-Cross-St, sc in next st; sk next 4 sts, FPdtr around each of next 3 sts, working behind FPdtr just made, hdc in 4th skipped st, working in front of FPdtr just made, FPdtr around each of first 3 skipped sts (beginning 3-Over-3 FPdtr-Cable made); sc in next st] 2 times, work beginning FPdc-Cross-St, sc in next st, work beginning 2-Over-2 FPtr-Cable over next 5 sts, sc in next st, work beginning FPdc-Cross-St, sc in last 2 sts, turn.

Note: From here on, all Cross-sts and Cables are worked around the posts of post stitches 2 rows below, instead of around stitches just 1 row below.

Row 2: Ch 1, sc in each st across, turn.

Row 3: Ch 1, sc in first 2 sts, [FPdc-Cross-St, sc in next st, FPdc around each of next 2 sts 2 rows below, hdc in next st, FPdc around each of next 2 sts 2 rows below, sc in next st, FPdc-Cross-St, sc in next st, FPdc around each of next 3 sts 2 rows below, hdc in next st, FPdc around each of next 3 sts 2 rows below, sc in next st] 2 times, FPdc-Cross-St, sc in next st, FPdc around each of next 2 sts 2 rows below, hdc in next st, FPdc around each of next 2 sts 2 rows below, sc in next sc, FPdc-Cross-St, sc in last 2 sts, turn.

Row 4: Ch 1, sc in each st across, turn.

Row 5: Ch 1, sc in first 2 sts, [FPdc-Cross-St, sc in next st, work 2-Over-2 FPtr-Cable over next 5 sts, sc in next st, FPdc-Cross-St, sc in next st, FPdc around each of next 3 sts 2 rows below, hdc in next st, FPdc around each of next 3 sts 2 rows below, sc in next st] 2 times, FPdc-Cross-St, sc in next st, work 2-Over-2 FPtr-Cable over next 5 sts, sc in next sc, FPdc-Cross-St, sc in last 2 sts, turn.

Rows 6–8: Repeat Rows 2–4.

Row 9: Ch 1, sc in first 2 sts, [FPdc-Cross-St, sc in next st, work 2-Over-2 FPtr-Cable over next 5 sts, sc in next st, FPdc-Cross-St, sc in next st, work 3-Over-3 FPdtr-Cable over next 7 sts, sc in next st] 2 times, FPdc-Cross-St, sc in next st, work 2-Over-2 FPtr-Cable over next 5 sts, sc in next sc, FPdc-Cross-St, sc in last 2 sts, turn.

Rows 10–14: Repeat Rows 2–6.

Row 15: Ch 1, sc in next 2 sts, [FPdc-Cross-St, sc in next st, FPdc around each of next 2 sts 2 rows below, hdc in next st, FPdc around each of next 2 sts 2 rows below, sc in next st, FPdc-Cross-St, sc in next st, FPdc around each of next 2 sts 2 rows below, 1-over-1 FPdc-Cable over next 3 sts, FPdc around next 2 sts 2 rows below, sc in next st] 2 times, FPdc-Cross-St, sc in next st, FPdc around each of next 2 sts 2 rows below, hdc in next st, FPdc around each of next 2 sts 2 rows below, sc in next sc, FPdc-Cross-St, sc in last 2 sts, turn.

Rows 16–24: Repeat Rows 4–12.

Row 25: Repeat Row 9.
Repeat Rows 2–25, 4 {5, 6, 6, 7, 8} more times.
Repeat Rows 2–24 {16, 8, 24, 16, 8} once more.
Note: You should have worked a total of 144 (160, 176, 192, 208, 224) rows.

FRONT
Fsc 75 {83, 95, 103, 112, 121}, turn.

Row 1 (RS): Ch 1, sc in first st; sc FLO in each st across to last st, sc in last st, turn.

Rows 2–72 {71, 71, 70, 70, 70}: Repeat Row 1.

SHAPE ARMHOLES
Row 1: Ch 1, sl st in first 6 {7, 11, 15, 18, 22} sts, ch 1, sc in next st; sc FLO in each st across to last 7 {8, 12, 16, 19, 23} sts; sc in next st, turn; leave remaining 6, {7,11,15,18, 22} sts unworked: 63 {69, 73, 73, 76, 77} sts.

Rows 2–19 {20, 22, 24, 25, 25}: Ch 1, sc in first st; sc FLO in each st across to last st, sc in last st, turn.

SHAPE NECK AND FIRST SHOULDER
Row 1 (WS): Ch 1, sc in first st; sc FLO in next 17 {19, 20, 20, 20, 20} sts; sc in next st, turn; leave remaining sts unworked for neck and second shoulder: 19 {21, 22, 22, 22, 22} sts

Rows 2–5: Ch 1, sc in first st; sc FLO in each st across to last st, sc in last st, turn.
Fasten off.

SHAPE SECOND SHOULDER
With WS facing, sk next 25 {27, 29, 29, 32, 33} unworked sts following first shoulder, join yarn with sl st in next st.

Row 1 (WS): Ch 1, sc in same st as join; sc FLO in each st across to last st, sc in last st, turn.

Rows 2–5: Ch 1, sc in first st; sc FLO in each st across to last st, sc in last st, turn.
Fasten off.

BACK
Make same as front.

SLEEVE (make 2)
Fsc 67 {67, 69, 69, 71, 71}.

Row 1: Ch 1, hdc in first st; hdc FLO in next 26 {26, 27, 27, 28, 28} sts, place a marker (pm) in last st made; hdc in next st, sk next st, tr in next st, tr in skipped st (beginning FPtr-Cross-St made), hdc in next st, sk next 3 sts, FPdtr around each of next 2 sts, working behind FPdtr just made, hdc in 3rd skipped st, working in front of FPdtr just made, FPdtr around each of first 2 skipped sts (beginning 2-Over-2 FPdtr Cable made), hdc in next st, work beginning FPtr-Cross-St, hdc in next st; pm in next st made, hdc FLO in each st across to last st; hdc in last st, turn.
Note: The markers indicate the 13 center stitches of the sleeve. The cable pattern for the sleeve is worked over these 13 stitches. Move the markers up as each row is worked.

Row 2: Ch 1, hdc in first st; hdc FLO in each st up to and including first marked st; hdc in next 13 sts; hdc FLO in each st across to last st; hdc in last st, turn.

Row 3: Ch 1, hdc in first st; hdc FLO in each st up to and including first marked st; hdc in next st, FPtr-Cross-st, hdc in next st, FPtr around each of next 2 sts, hdc in next st, FPtr around each of next 2 sts, hdc in next st, FPtr-Cross-st, hdc in next st; hdc FLO in each st across to last st; hdc in last st, turn.

Row 4: Repeat Row 2.

Row 5: Ch 1, hdc in first st; hdc FLO in each st up to and including first marked st; hdc in next st, FPtr-Cross-st, hdc in next st, 2-Over-2 FPdtr Cable, hdc in next st, FPtr-Cross-St, hdc in next st; hdc FLO in each st across to last st; hdc in last st, turn.

Row 6: Repeat Row 2.

Rows 7–58 {58, 62, 62, 66, 70}: Repeat last 4 rows 13 {13, 14, 14, 15, 16} more times.

Row 59 {59, 63, 63, 67, 71}: Repeat Row 3.

SHAPE CAP
Row 1: Ch 1, hdc in first st; [hdc2tog FLO] twice, hdc FLO in each st across to last 5 sts, [hdc2tog FLO] twice; hdc in last st, turn: 63 (63, 65, 65, 67, 67) sts.

Row 2: Ch 1, hdc in first st; [hdc2tog FLO] twice, hdc FLO in each st up to and including marked st; hdc in next st, FPtr-Cross-St, hdc in next st, 2-Over-2 FPdtr Cable, hdc in next st, FPtr-Cross-St, hdc in next st; hdc FLO in each st across to last 5 sts, [hdc2tog FLO] twice; hdc in last st, turn: 59 {59, 61, 61, 63, 63} sts.

Row 3: Repeat Row 1: 55 {55, 57, 57, 59, 59} sts.

Row 4: Ch 1, hdc in first st; [hdc2tog FLO] twice, hdc FLO in each st up to and including marked st; hdc in next st, FPtr-Cross-St, hdc in next st, FPtr around each of next 2 sts, hdc in next st, FPtr around each of next 2 sts, hdc in next st, FPtr-Cross-St, hdc in next st; hdc FLO in each st across to last 5 sts, [hdc2tog FLO] twice; hdc in last st, turn: 51 {51, 53, 53, 55, 55} sts.

Rows 5–8: Repeat last 4 rows once more: 35 {35, 37, 37, 39, 39} sts.

Rows 9–11: Repeat Rows 1–3: 23 {23, 25, 25, 27, 27} sts.

Row 12: Ch 1, hdc in first st; [hdc2tog FLO] 1 {1, 2, 2, 2, 2} time(s), hdc FLO in each st up to and including marked st; hdc in next st, FPtr-Cross-St, hdc in next st, FPtr around each of next 2 sts, hdc in next st, FPtr around each of next 2 sts, hdc in next st, FPtr-Cross-St, hdc in next st; hdc FLO in each st across to last 3 {3, 5, 5, 5, 5} sts, [hdc2tog FLO] 1 {1, 2, 2, 2, 2} time(s); hdc in last st, turn: 21 {21, 21, 21, 23, 23} sts.

Row 13: Ch 1, hdc in first st; [hdc2tog FLO] 1 {1, 1, 1, 2, 2} times(s), hdc FLO in each st across to last 3 {3, 3, 3, 5, 5} sts, [hdc2tog FLO] 1 {1, 1, 1, 2, 2} time(s); hdc in last st, turn: 19 sts.

Row 14: Ch 1, hdc in first st; hdc2tog FLO, hdc FLO in each st up to and including marked st; hdc in next st, FPtr-Cross-St, hdc in next st, 2-Over-2 FPdtr Cable, hdc in next st, FPtr-Cross-St, hdc in next st; hdc FLO in each st across to 3 sts, hdc2tog FLO; hdc in last st, turn: 17 sts.

Row 15: Ch 1, hdc in first st; hdc2tog FLO, hdc FLO in each st across to last 3 sts, hdc2tog FLO; hdc in last st, turn: 15 sts.

Row 16: Ch 1, hdc in first st; hdc2tog FLO, hdc FLO in each st up to and including marked st; hdc in next st, FPtr-Cross-St, hdc in next st, FPtr around each of next 2 sts, hdc in next st, FPtr around each of next 2 sts, hdc in next st, FPtr-Cross-St, hdc in next st; hdc FLO in each st across to 3 sts, hdc2tog FLO; hdc in last st, turn: 13 sts.

SADDLE SHOULDER

Row 1: Repeat Row 2 of sleeve.

Row 2: Repeat Row 5 of sleeve.

Rows 3 and 4: Repeat Rows 2 and 3 of sleeve.

Rows 5–12: Repeat last 4 rows 2 more times.

Rows 13 and 14: Repeat Rows 4 and 5 of sleeve.

Repeat Row 2 of sleeve 0 {1, 1, 1, 1, 1} time(s).

Repeat Row 3 of sleeve 0 {0, 1, 1, 1, 1} time(s).
Fasten off.

FINISHING
Block pieces to schematic measurements. Beginning at neckline, sew shoulder and armhole seams. Sew side and sleeve seams. Sew ends of lower cable section together to form a tube. Sew lower cable section to main body, attaching at Row 34 of body; this creates the lining for the lower portion of the tunic.

COWL NECK
Round 1 (RS): With RS facing, join yarn with sl st in shoulder seam, hdc evenly spaced around neck edge; do not join, work in continuous spirals. Place marker for beginning of round and move marker up as each round is completed.

Rounds 2–22: Working in back loops only, hdc in each st around.
Fasten off.
Weave in ends.

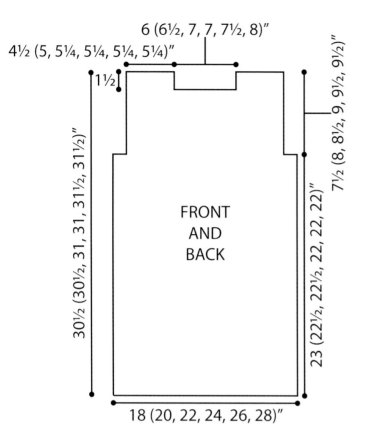

6 (6½, 7, 7, 7½, 8)"

4½ (5, 5¼, 5¼, 5¼, 5¼)"

1½

30½ (30½, 31, 31, 31½, 31½)"

FRONT
AND
BACK

7½ (8, 8½, 9, 9½, 9½)"

23 (22½, 22½, 22, 22, 22)"

18 (20, 22, 24, 26, 28)"

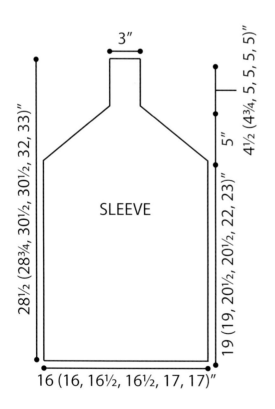

3"

28½ (28¾, 30½, 30½, 32, 33)"

4½ (4¾, 5, 5, 5, 5)"

5"

SLEEVE

19 (19, 20½, 20½, 22, 23)"

16 (16, 16½, 16½, 17, 17)"

Rio de Janeiro

I love hoodies. To me, a hoodie is the go-to piece for versatility in just about any wardrobe. For this design, I combined the look of a hoodie with the added layering possibilities of a vest and worked the entire piece up in an easy stitch that lays flat without adding bulk to your look. I finished the design with draped front panels for a little laid back chic.

SKILL LEVEL: ⬛⬛◻◻ **EASY**

SIZE: Small {Medium, Large, 1X, 2X, 3X}

FINISHED MEASUREMENTS:
To Fit Bust: 34 {38, 42, 46, 50, 54}" / 86.5 {96.5, 106.5, 117, 126, 137} cm
Length: 17½ {18, 18½, 19, 19½, 20}" / 44.5 {45.5, 47, 48.5, 49.5, 51} cm

SIZE NOTE:
Instructions are written for Small size with changes for larger sizes in braces { }. Instructions will be easier to read if you circle all the numbers pertaining to your size. If only one number is given it pertains to all sizes.

MATERIALS
Light Weight Yarn 〔3〕 LIGHT
[1.75 ounces, 150 yards (50 grams, 137 meters) per ball]: 7 {9, 10, 11, 12, 13} balls
Shown In: Malabrigo Silky Merino (50% Silk/50% Merino Wool; 1.75oz/50g, 150yds/137m): Color #27 Bobby Blue
Crochet Hook: Size F-5 (3.75 mm) **or** size needed for Gauge
Yarn Needle

BLOCKED GAUGE:
In pattern, 20 sts = 4" (10 cm) and 16 rows = 4" (10 cm).

GAUGE SWATCH: Block to 7 x 6" (18 x 15 cm)
Fhdc 35, turn.

Rows 1–24: Ch 1, sc in first st, sc FLO in each st across to last st, sc in last st, turn.
Fasten off.

STITCH GUIDE

Foundation Half Double Crochet (Fhdc):
Ch 2, yo, insert hook in 2nd ch from hook, yo and draw up a loop, yo and draw through 1 loop (first "chain" made), yo and draw through 3 loops on hook (first hdc made), ✳ yo, insert hook under 2 loops of the "chain" just made, yo and draw up a loop, yo and draw through 1 loop ("chain" made), yo and draw through 3 loops on hook (hdc made); repeat from ✳ for desired number of foundation stitches.
(See page 94)

Notes:
1. This stitch pattern is reversible and, therefore, should look the same on both sides of the fabric. When instructed to work from RS, select whichever side you like best as the RS.

2. Body is worked in one piece from lower edge up to the underarm. The piece is then divided for armholes, and back and fronts worked separately.

Rio Sleeveless Hoodie 🖎

BODY
Fsc 285 {305, 325, 345, 365, 385}, turn.

Row 1: Ch 1, sc in first st, sc FLO in each st across to last st, sc in last st, turn.

Rows 2–12: Repeat Row 1 eleven more times.

Row 13: Ch 1, sc in first st, sc2tog FLO, sc FLO in each st across to last 3 sts, sc2tog FLO, sc in last st, turn: 283 {303, 323, 343, 363, 383} sts.

Rows 14–41: Repeat Row 13 twenty-eight more times: 227 {247, 267, 287, 307, 327} sts.

DIVIDE FOR ARMHOLES
FIRST FRONT
Row 1: Ch 1, sc in first st, sc2tog FLO, sc FLO in next 67 {73, 79, 85, 91, 97} sts, sc in next st, turn; leave rem sts unworked (for armholes, back, and second front): 70 {76, 82, 88, 94, 100} sts.

Row 2: Ch 1, sc in first st, sc2tog FLO, sc FLO in each st across to last 3 sts, sc2tog FLO, sc in last st, turn: 68 {74, 80, 86, 92, 98} sts.

Row 3: Ch 1, sc in first st, sc2tog FLO, sc FLO in each st across to last st, sc in last st, turn: 67 {73, 79, 85, 91, 97} sts.

Rows 4–21 {23, 27, 31, 33, 35}: Repeat last 2 rows 9 {10, 12, 14, 15, 16} more times: 40 {43, 43, 43, 46, 49} sts.

Row 22 {24, 28, 32, 34, 36}: Ch 1, sc in first st, sc FLO in each st across to last 3 sts, sc2tog FLO, sc in last st, turn: 39 {42, 42, 42, 45, 48} sts.

Row 23 {25, 29, 33, 35, 37}: Ch 1, sc in first st, sc2tog FLO, sc FLO in each st across to last st, sc in last st, turn: 38 {41, 41, 41, 44, 47} sts.

Repeat last 2 rows 2 {2, 0, 0, 0, 0} more times: 34 {37, 41, 41, 44, 47} sts.

Next Row: Repeat Row 22 {24, 28, 32, 34, 36}: 33 {36, 40, 40, 43, 46} sts.
Fasten off.

BACK
Sk 0 {0, 0, 2, 4, 6} unworked sts following Row 1 of first front, join yarn in next unworked st.

Row 1: Ch 1, sc in same st as join, sc FLO in next 83 {91, 99, 103, 107, 111} sts, sc in next st, turn; leave rem sts unworked (for armhole and second front): 85 {93, 101, 105, 109, 113} sts.

Row 2: Ch 1, sc in first st, sc2tog FLO, sc FLO in each st across to last 3 sts, sc2tog FLO, sc in last st, turn: 83 {91, 99, 103, 107, 111} sts.

Row 3: Ch 1, sc in first st, sc FLO in each st across, sc in last st, turn.

Rows 4–21 {23, 27, 31, 33, 35}: Repeat last 2 rows 9 {10, 12, 14, 15, 16} more times: 65 {71, 75, 75, 77, 79} sts.

Row 22 {24, 28, 32, 34, 36}: Ch 1, sc in first st, sc FLO in each st across to last st, sc in last st, turn. Rep last row until back measures same as first front. Fasten off.

SECOND FRONT
Sk 0 {0, 0, 2, 4, 6} unworked sts following Row 1 of back, join yarn in next unworked st.

Row 1: Ch 1, sc in same st as join, sc FLO in each st across to last 3 sts, sc2tog FLO, sc in last st, turn: 70 {76, 82, 88, 94, 100} sts.

Row 2: Ch 1, sc in first st, sc2tog FLO, sc FLO in each st across to last 3 sts, sc2tog FLO, sc in last st, turn: 68 {74, 80, 86, 92, 98} sts.

Row 3: Ch 1, sc in first st, sc FLO in each st across to last 3 sts, sc2tog FLO, sc in last st, turn: 67 {73, 79, 85, 91, 97} sts.

Rows 4–21 {23, 27, 31, 33, 35}: Repeat last 2 rows 9 {10, 12, 14, 15, 16} more times: 40 {43, 43, 43, 46, 49} sts.

Row 22 {24, 28, 32, 34, 36}: Ch 1, sc in first st, sc2tog FLO, sc FLO in each st across to last st, sc in last st, turn: 39 {42, 42, 42, 45, 48} sts.

Row 23 {25, 29, 33, 35, 37}: Ch 1, sc in first st, sc FLO in each st across to last 3 sts, sc2tog FLO, sc in last st, turn: 38 {41, 41, 41, 44, 47} sts.

Repeat last 2 rows 2 {2, 0, 0, 0, 0} more times: 34 {37, 41, 41, 44, 47} sts.

Next Row: Repeat Row 22 {24, 28, 32, 34, 36}: 33 {36, 40, 40, 43, 46} sts.
Fasten off.

HOOD
Block piece to schematic measurements. Sew 4 {4, 4 1/2, 4 1/2, 5, 5 1/2}" / 10 {10, 11.5, 11.5, 12.5, 12.5} cm shoulder seam in preparation for stitching hood. Join yarn with sl st in first st at top front corner, to work across neck edge.

Row 1: Ch 1, sc in same st as join, sc FLO in each st across neck edge to opposite top corner, sc in last st at opposite corner, turn.

Rows 2–50: Ch 1, sc in first st, sc FLO in each st across, sc in last st, turn.
Fasten off, leaving a long tail for sewing.

Fold hood in half. With RS facing, sew top edges together (across Row 50).

FINISHING
Front Border

With RS facing, join yarn with sl st in lower front corner, to work up front edge.

Row 1: Ch 1, hdc in same sp as join, hdc evenly spaced up front edge, around hood edge, and down other front edge to opposite lower corner, turn.

Rows 2–13: Ch 1, hdc in first st, hdc BLO in each st across to last st, hdc in last st, turn.
Fasten off.

Armhole Edging

With RS facing, join yarn with sl st in underarm, to work around armhole.

Round 1: Ch 1, sc in same sp as join, sc evenly spaced around armhole edge; join with sl st in first sc. Fasten off.
Note: If sc border sts are too tight and gather or restrict the edges of the fabric, use Split-Sc Border or Hdc Border instead. (See page 93)

Weave in ends.

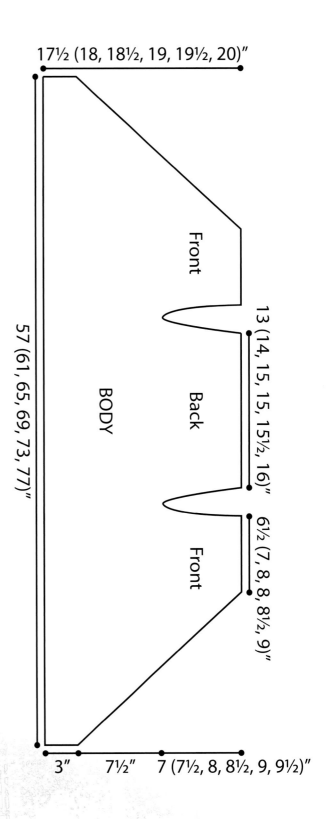

17½ (18, 18½, 19, 19½, 20)"

Front

Back

Front

BODY

13 (14, 15, 15, 15½, 16)"

6½ (7, 8, 8, 8½, 9)"

57 (61, 65, 69, 73, 77)"

3"   7½"   7 (7½, 8, 8½, 9, 9½)"

St. Tropez

In every hustle and bustle, there are the quiet moments we take. I designed this top with a nod to the softer side of the city. The easy fit of this top and the butterfly feature of the sleeves are soft, feminine and flattering on most body types. Urban professionals, weekend window shoppers and soccer moms alike will all find this piece the perfect soft balance to the rigors of the urban jungle.

SKILL LEVEL: ◼◼◻◻ **EASY**

SIZE: Small {Medium, Large, 1X, 2X, 3X}

FINISHED MEASUREMENTS:
To Fit Bust: 34 {38, 42, 46, 50, 54}" / 86.5 {96.5, 106.5, 117, 127, 137} cm
Length: 23½ {23¾, 24, 24¼, 24¾, 25}" / 59.5 {60.5, 61, 61.5, 63, 63.5} cm

SIZE NOTE:
Instructions are written for Small size with changes for larger sizes in braces { }. Instructions will be easier to read if you circle all the numbers pertaining to your size. If only one number is given it pertains to both sizes.

MATERIALS
Light Weight Yarn 🧶 LIGHT 3
[3 ounces, 251 yards (85 grams, 230 meters) per ball]: 5 {5, 6, 7, 7, 8} balls
Shown In: Naturally Caron.com SPA (75% Microdenier Acrylic/25% Rayon from bamboo; 3oz/85g, 251yds/230m): Color #0014 Rosalind
Crochet Hook: Size F-5 (3.75 mm) **or** size needed foH Gauge
Yarn Needle

BLOCKED GAUGE: In Star St Pattern, 28 sts = 5" (12.5 cm) and 14 rows = 5" (12.5 cm).

GAUGE SWATCH: Block to 5 x 5" (12.5 x 12.5 cm) square
Fsc 28, turn.

Work in Star St Pattern for 14 rows: 14 Stars.
Fasten off

Star Stitch Pattern

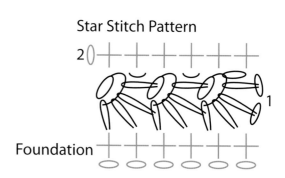

STITCH GUIDE

Foundation Single Crochet (Fsc): Ch 2, insert hook in 2nd ch from hook, yo and draw up a loop, yo and draw through 1 loop (first "chain" made), yo and draw through 2 loops on hook (first sc made), ✳ insert hook under 2 loops of the "chain" just made, yo and draw up a loop, yo and draw through 1 loop ("chain" made), yo and draw through 2 loops on hook (sc made); repeat from ✳ for desired number of foundation stitches. **(See page 94)**

First Star Stitch: Ch 3, insert hook in 2nd ch from hook (skipped ch is arm of first Star), yo and draw up a loop, insert hook in next ch, yo and draw up a loop (3 loops on hook), [insert hook in next sc, yo and draw up a loop] 2 times (5 loops on hook), yo and draw through all 5 loops on hook, ch 1 to close Star and form eye.

Star Stitch (Star St): Insert hook in eye of last Star made, yo and draw up a loop, insert hook into back of 5th loop of last Star made, yo and draw up a loop (3 loops on hook), [insert hook in next st, yo and draw up a loop] 2 times (5 loops on hook), yo and draw through all 5 loops on hook, ch 1 to close Star and form eye of Star.

Note: Loop that is on hook when a Star Stitch is started forms the arm of the Star. In Star St Pattern, a stitch is worked into the eye and arm of each star.

Star Stitch Pattern (multiple of 2 sts)
Row 1 (RS): First Star, work Star st across, turn.

Row 2: Ch 1, sc in eye of first Star, ✳ sc FLO in next st (arm of Star), sc in eye of next Star; repeat from ✳ across to last st, sc in last st, turn. Rep Rows 1 and 2 for Star St pattern.

St. Tropez Butterfly Sleeve Top ⋙

BODY PANEL (make 2)

Fsc 96 {106, 118, 128, 140, 150}, turn.

Row 1 (RS): First Star, work Star St across, turn: 48 {53, 59, 64, 70, 75} Stars.

Row 2: Ch 1, sc in eye of first Star, sc FLO in next st (arm of Star), ✳ sc in eye of next Star, sc FLO in next st; repeat from ✳ across to last st, sc in last st, turn: 96 {106, 118, 128, 140, 150} sc.

Continue in Star St Pattern until piece measures 16½ {16¼, 16, 15¾, 15¾, 15½}" / 42 {41.5, 40.5, 40, 40, 39.5} cm from beginning, end with a WS row.

SHAPE ARMHOLES

Row 1: Ch 1, sk first sc, sl st in next sc, work in Star St Pattern across to last 2 sts, turn; leave last 2 sts unworked: 46 {51, 57, 62, 68, 73} Stars.

Row 2: Ch 1, sk eye of first star, sk next st, ✳ sc in eye of next Star, sc FLO in next st; repeat from ✳ across to last 2 sts, turn; leave last 2 sts unworked: 88 {98, 110, 120, 132, 142} sc.

Rows 3–12 {12, 14, 16, 20, 22}: Repeat last 2 rows 5 {5, 6, 7, 9, 10} times: 48 {58, 62, 64, 60, 62} sc.

Repeat Row 1, 1 {1, 1, 1, 0, 0} time(s): 22 {27, 29, 30, 30, 31} Stars.

Continue even in Star St Pattern until armhole measures 7 {7½, 8, 8½, 9, 9½}" / 18 {19, 20.5, 21.5, 23, 24} cm, end with a WS row. Fasten off.

SLEEVE (make 2)

Fsc 78 {82, 88, 94, 100, 104}, turn.

Row 1 (RS): First Star, work Star St across, turn: 39 {41, 44, 47, 50, 52} Stars.

Row 2: Ch 1, sc in eye of first Star, sc FLO in next st, ✳ sc in eye of next Star, sc FLO in next st; repeat from ✳ across to last st, sc in last st, turn: 78 {82, 88, 94, 100, 104} sc.

Continue in Star St Pattern until piece measures 8 {8, 8½, 8½, 9, 9}" / 20.5 {20.5, 21.5, 21.5, 23, 23} cm from beginning, end with a WS row.

SHAPE FIRST HALF OF CAP

Note: Cap is worked in two halves, on either side of center of sleeve. This results in a 'V' shape cut-out at the center top of the sleeve.

Row 1: Continue in Star St Pattern over first 36 {38, 40, 42, 44, 46} sts, turn; leave remaining sts unworked (for underarm and 2nd half of cap): 18 {19, 20, 21, 22, 23} Stars.

Row 2: Ch 1, sk eye of first Star, sl st in next st, sl st in eye of next Star, ch 1, sc FLO in next st, ✳ sc in eye of next Star, sc FLO in next st; repeat from ✳ across, turn: 33 {35, 37, 39, 41, 43} sc.

Row 3: Continue in Star St Pattern across to last 3 sts, turn; leave last 3 sts unworked: 15 {16, 17, 18, 19, 20} Stars.

Rows 4–11 {13, 13, 13, 15, 15}: Repeat last 2 rows 4 {5, 5, 5, 6, 6} times: 3 {1, 2, 3, 1, 2} Star(s).

Sizes S {1X} Only
Row 12 {14}: Repeat Row 2: 3 sc.

Row 13 {15}: Ch 1, sc in first 2 sc, turn; leave last st unworked: 2 sc.

Sizes M {2X} Only
Row 14 {16}: Ch 1, sc in each st across, turn: 2 sc.

Row 14 {16}: Ch 1, sk eye of first Star, sc in next 3 sts, turn: 3 sc.

Row 15 {17}: Ch 1, sc in first 2 sc, turn; leave last st unworked: 2 sc.

All Sizes

Last Row: Ch 1, sc in first sc, sc in next sc. Fasten off.

SHAPE SECOND HALF OF CAP

Row 1: Sk next 6 {8, 8, 10, 12, 12} unworked sts following Row 1 of first half of cap, join yarn with sl st in next st, work Row 1 of Star St Pattern over last 36 {38, 40, 42, 44, 46} sts, turn: 18 {19, 20, 21, 22, 23} Stars.

Row 2: Continue in Star St Pattern across to last 3 sts, turn; leave last 3 sts unworked: 33 {35, 37, 39, 41, 43} sc.

Row 3: Ch 1, sk eye of first Star, sl st in next st, sl st in eye of next Star, ch 1, sc FLO in next st, ✳ sc in eye of next Star, sc FLO in next st; repeat from ✳ across: 15 {16, 17, 18, 19, 20} Stars.

Rows 4–11 {13, 13, 13, 15, 15}: Repeat last 2 rows 4 {5, 5, 5, 6, 6} times: 3 {1, 2, 3, 1, 2} Star(s).

Sizes S {1X} Only

Row 12 {14}: Repeat Row 2: 3 sc.

Row 13 {15}: Ch 1, sk first sc, sc in last 2 sc, turn: 2 sc.

Sizes M {2X} Only

Row 14 {16}: Ch 1, sc in each st across, turn: 2 sc.

Sizes L {3X} Only

Row 14 {16}: Ch 1, sc in first 3 sts, turn; leave last st unworked: 3 sc.

Row 15 {17}: Ch 1, sk first sc, sc in last 2 sc, turn: 2 sc.

All Sizes

Last Row: Ch 1, sc in first sc, sc in next sc. Fasten off.

FINISHING

Block pieces to schematic measurements. Sew side seams. Sew sleeve seams, beginning at cuff edge and sewing for 1–3" / 2.5–7.5 cm. Leave top of sleeve unsewn, for butterfly opening.

Set-in Sleeves: Pin sleeve into armhole, placing bottom of 'V' centered at underarm. Sew side edges of 'V' to armhole edges. Sew tips of 'V' together and to top corners of body panels. Weave in ends.

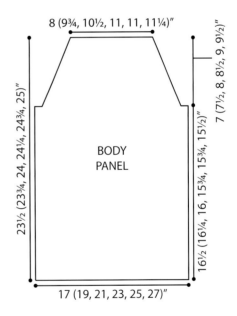

8 (9¾, 10½, 11, 11, 11¼)"

7 (7½, 8, 8½, 9, 9½)"

23½ (23¾, 24, 24¼, 24¾, 25)"

BODY PANEL

16½ (16¼, 16, 15¾, 15¾, 15½)"

17 (19, 21, 23, 25, 27)"

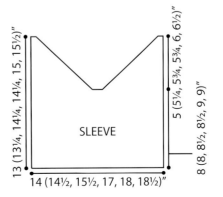

13 (13¼, 14¼, 14¼, 15, 15½)"

5 (5¼, 5¾, 5¾, 6, 6½)"

SLEEVE

8 (8, 8½, 8½, 9, 9)"

14 (14½, 15½, 17, 18, 18½)"

Buenos Aires

I believe every woman deserves to put a little pizzazz in her wardrobe. I used a classic filet crochet stitch pattern to build this twist on a classic duster silhouette. The result is a fun layering piece with the versatility of a vest and the added drama of a duster. The Buenos Aires Maxi Vest will look FAB with your jeans, slacks or skirts, tanks, tees, turtlenecks and button-up shirts.

SKILL LEVEL: ◼◼◼◻ INTERMEDIATE

SIZE: Small {Medium, Large, 1X, 2X, 3X}

FINISHED MEASUREMENTS:
To Fit Bust: 34 {38, 42, 46, 50, 54}" / 86.5 {96.5, 106.5, 117, 127, 137} cm
Length: 43 {43$\frac{1}{2}$, 44$\frac{1}{2}$, 44$\frac{1}{2}$, 44$\frac{1}{2}$, 45}" / 109 {110.5, 113, 113, 113, 114.5} cm

SIZE NOTE:
Instructions are written for Small size with changes for larger sizes in braces { }. Instructions will be easier to read if you circle all the numbers pertaining to your size. If only one number is given it pertains to all sizes.

MATERIALS
Light Weight Yarn
[1.75 ounces, 108 yards (50 grams, 100 meters) per ball]: 13 {14, 16, 17, 19, 21} balls
Shown In: Tahki Cotton Classic (100% Mercerized Cotton; 1.75oz/50g, 108yds/100m): Color #3913 Dark Red-Violet
Crochet Hook: size E-4 (3.5 mm) **or** size needed for Gauge
Crochet Hook: size F-5 (3.75 mm) (for front and armhole eging)
Yarn Needle

BLOCKED GAUGE: In Lace Pattern, 18 sts = 4 $^{3}/_{4}$" (12 cm) and 14 rows = 5 $^{3}/_{4}$" (14.5 cm) with smaller hook

GAUGE SWATCH: Block to 5$\frac{1}{2}$ x 5$^{3}/_{4}$" (14 x 14.5 cm) square
Fsc 21, turn.
Work in Lace Pattern for 14 rows.
Fasten off.

STITCH GUIDE

Foundation Single Crochet (Fsc): Ch 2, insert hook in 2nd ch from hook, yo and draw up a loop, yo and draw through 1 loop (first "chain" made), yo and draw through 2 loops on hook (first sc made), * insert hook under 2 loops of the "chain" just made, yo and draw up a loop, yo and draw through 1 loop ("chain" made), yo and draw through 2 loops on hook (sc made); repeat from * for desired number of foundation stitches. *(See page 94)*

First Double Crochet (First-Dc): Sc in first st, ch 2.

Note: This stitch replaces the more common ch-3 at the beginning of rows and produces a flatter edge.

Y-stitch (Y-St): Tr in indicated st, ch 3, dc in side of tr just made.

Note: To work in the side of the tr insert your hook into the first horizontal loop just above the base of the tr.

Beginning Y-stitch (Beg Y-St): Ch 6 (counts as tr, ch 2), dc in 5th ch from hook.

Ending Y-stitch (End Y-St): Tr in indicated st, ch 2, dc in side of tr just made.

Lace Pattern (multiple of 4 sts + 1)
Row 1 (RS): Ch 1, sc in each st across, turn.

Row 2: Ch 1, hdc in each st across, turn.

Row 3: Repeat Row 1.

Row 4: Ch 1, sc in first st, Beg Y-St, * sk next 3 sts, Y-St in next st; repeat from * across to last 4 sts, sk next 3 sts, End Y-St in last st, turn.

Rows 5 and 6: Ch 1, sc in first st, Beg Y-St, * Y-St in ch-3 sp of next Y-St; repeat from * across to Beg Y-St, sk next 2 ch of Beg Y-St, end Y-St in next ch, turn.

Row 7: Ch 1, sc in first dc, ch 1, sk next ch-2 sp, hdc in next sp between Y-Sts, * ch 1, sc in next ch-3 sp, ch 1, hdc in next sp between Y-Sts; repeat from * across to Beg Y-St, ch 1, sk next 2 ch of Beg Y-St, sc in next ch, turn.

Row 8: Ch 1, hdc in each st and ch-1 across, turn.

Rows 9–12: Repeat Rows 1–4.

Row 13: Ch 1, sc in first dc, ch 3, sk next ch-2 sp, sc in next ch-3 sp, * ch 3, sc in next ch-3 sp; repeat from * across to Beg Y-st, sk next 2 ch of Beg Y-st, sc in next ch, turn.

Row 14: First-dc, 3 dc in next ch-3 sp, * ch 1, sk next sc, 3 dc in next ch-3 sp; repeat from * across to last sc, dc in last sc, turn.

Row 15: First-dc, dc in next dc, * ch 1, sk next dc, dc in next dc, dc in next ch-1 sp, dc in next dc; repeat from * across to last 3 sts, ch 1, sk next dc, dc in last 2 sts, turn.

Row 16: First-dc, dc in next dc, dc in next ch-1 sp, dc in next dc, * ch 1, sk next dc, dc in next dc, dc in next ch-1 sp, dc in next dc; repeat from * across to last st, dc in last st, turn.

Rows 17 and 18: Repeat Rows 15 and 16.

Row 19–23: Repeat Rows 8–12.

Rows 24–26: Repeat Rows 7–9.

Row 27: First-dc, * ch 1, sk next st, dc in next st; repeat from * across, turn.

Row 28: Ch 1, sc in first st, * ch 1, sk next ch-1 sp, sc FLO in next dc; repeat from * across to last st, sc in last st, turn.

Row 29: First dc, * ch 1, sk next ch-1 sp, dc in next st; repeat from * across, turn.

Rows 30 and 31: Repeat Rows 28 and 29.

Rows 32–35: Repeat Rows 8–11.

Notes:

1. Body is worked in one piece from lower edge up to the underarm. The piece is then divided for armholes, and back and fronts worked separately.

2. Stitches are skipped at waist, to form two darts. The excess fabric is folded into pleats and the top opening sewn closed to form back darts, during finishing.

Buenos Aires Maxi Vest ☞

BODY
Fhdc 193 {209, 225, 241, 254, 271}, turn.

Rows 1–35 (RS): Work Rows 1–35 of Lace Pattern.

Rows 36–64: Work Rows 4–32 of Lace Pattern.

SHAPE DARTS
Row 65: Ch 1, sc in first 48 {52, 56, 60, 63, 67} sts, sk next 32 sts (for first dart), sc in next 33 {41, 49, 57, 64, 73} sts, sk next 32 sts (for second dart), sc in last 48 {52, 56, 60, 63, 67} sts, turn: 129 {145, 161, 177, 190, 207} sts.
Note: Leave skipped sts unworked. The fabric around the openings will be folded to form darts when finishing.

Rows 66–85: Work Rows 2–21 of Lace Pattern.

Lace Pattern

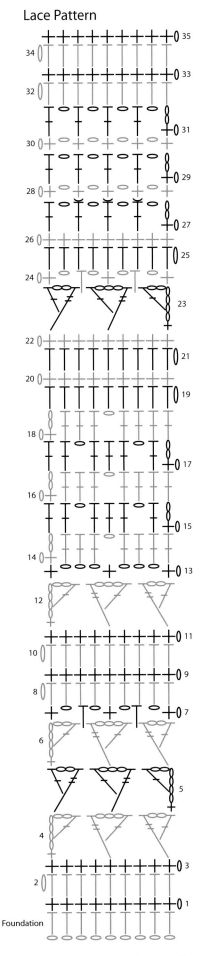

DIVIDE FOR ARMHOLES
FIRST FRONT

Row 86 (WS): Ch 1, sc in first 29 {33, 36, 40, 42, 47} sts, turn; leave remaining sts unworked (for armholes, back and second front): 29 {33, 36, 40, 42, 47} sts.

Rows 87 and 88: Work Rows 23 and 24 of Lace pattern.

SHAPE NECK

Row 89 (RS): Ch 1, hdc in each st and ch-1 across to last 3 sts, hdc2tog, hdc in last st, turn: 28 {32, 35, 39, 41, 46} sts.

Row 90: Ch 1, sc in first st, sc2tog, sc in each st across, turn: 27 {31, 34, 38, 40, 45} sts.

Row 91: First-dc, ✳ ch 1, sk next st, dc in next st; repeat from ✳ across to last 2 sts, sk next st, dc in last st, turn: 26 {30, 33, 37, 39, 44} sts.

Row 92: Ch 1, sc2tog, ✳ ch 1, sk next ch-1 sp, sc FLO in next dc; repeat from ✳ across to last ch-1 sp, ch 1, sk last ch-1 sp, sc in last st, turn: 25 {29, 32, 36, 38, 43} sts.

Row 93: Repeat Row 91: 24 {28, 31, 35, 37, 42} sts.

Rows 94 and 95: Repeat Rows 92 and 93: 22 {26, 29, 33, 35, 40} sts at the end of Row 95.

Row 96: Ch 1, hdc in first st, hdc2tog, hdc in each st across, turn: 21 {25, 28, 32, 34, 39} sts.

Row 97: Ch 1, sc in each st across to last 3 sts, sc2tog, sc in last st, turn: 20 {24, 27, 31, 33, 38} sts.

Rows 98–99 {101, 103, 103, 103, 105}: Repeat last 2 rows 1 (2, 3, 3, 3, 4) more times: 18 {20, 21, 25, 27, 30} sts at the end of last row.

Row 100 {102, 104, 104, 104, 106}: Ch 1, dc2tog, ✳ ch 1, sk next st, dc in next st; repeat from ✳ across, turn: 17 {19, 20, 24, 26, 29} sts.

Row 101 {103, 105, 105, 105, 107}: Ch 1, hdc in each st and ch-1 across, turn.

Rows 102 {104, 106, 106, 106, 108}–104 {106, 108, 108, 108, 110}: Work Rows 1–3 of Lace Pattern. Fasten off.

BACK

With WS facing, sk next 7 {7, 9, 9, 11, 11} unworked sts following first front, join yarn in next st.

Row 86 (WS): Ch 1, sc in same st as join, sc in next 56 {64, 70, 78, 83, 90} sts, turn; leave remaining sts unworked (for armhole and second front): 57 {65, 71, 79, 84, 91} sts.

Rows 87–99: Work Rows 23–35 of Lace Pattern. Repeat Rows 32 and 33 of Lace pattern 0 (1, 2, 2, 2, 3) more times.

Row 100 {102, 104, 104, 104, 106}: Work Row 27 of Lace pattern.

SHAPE FIRST SHOULDER

Row 101 {103, 105, 105, 105, 107}: Ch 1, hdc in first 17 {19, 20, 24, 26, 29} sts, turn; leave remaining sts unworked (for neck and second shoulder): 17 {19, 20, 24, 26, 29} sts.

Rows 102 {104, 106, 106, 106, 108}–104 {106, 108, 108, 108, 110}: Work Rows 1–3 of Lace Pattern. Fasten off.

SHAPE SECOND SHOULDER
With RS facing, sk next 23 {27, 31, 31, 32, 33} unworked sts following first shoulder, join yarn in next st.

Row 101 {103, 105, 105, 105, 107}: Ch 1, hdc in same st as join, hdc in next 16 {18, 19, 23, 25, 28} sts, turn: 17 {19, 20, 24, 26, 29} sts.

Rows 102 {104, 106, 106, 106, 108}–104 {106, 108, 108, 108, 110}: Work Rows 1–3 of Lace pattern. Fasten off.

SECOND FRONT
With WS facing, sk next 7 {7, 9, 9, 11, 11} unworked sts following back, join yarn in next st.

Row 86 (WS): Ch 1, sc in same st as join, sc in next 28 {32, 35, 39, 41, 46} sts, turn: 29 {33, 36, 40, 42, 47} sts.

Rows 87 and 88: Work Rows 23 and 24 of Lace pattern.

SHAPE NECK
Row 89 (RS): Ch 1, hdc in first st, hdc2tog, hdc in each st and ch-1 across, turn: 28 {32, 35, 39, 41, 46} sts.

Row 90: Ch 1, sc in each st across to last 3 sts, sc2tog, sc in last st, turn: 27 {31, 34, 38, 40, 45} sts.

Row 91: First-dc, sk next st, dc in next st, ✳ ch 1, sk next st, dc in next st; repeat from ✳ across, turn: 26 {30, 33, 37, 39, 44} sts.

Row 92: Ch 1, sc in first st, v ch 1, sk next ch-1 sp, sc FLO in next dc; repeat from v across to last ch-1 sp, ch 1, sk last ch-1 sp, sc2tog, turn: 25 {29, 32, 36, 38, 43} sts.

Row 93: Repeat Row 91: 24 {28, 31, 35, 37, 42} sts.

Rows 94 and 95: Repeat Rows 92 and 93: 22 {26, 29, 33, 35, 40} sts at the end of Row 95.

Row 96: Ch 1, hdc in each st and ch-1 across to last 3 sts, hdc2tog, hdc in last st, turn: 21 {25, 28, 32, 34, 39} sts.

Row 97: Ch 1, sc in first st, sc2tog, sc in each st across, turn: 20 {24, 27, 31, 33, 38} sts.

Rows 98–99 {101, 103, 103, 103, 105}: Repeat last 2 rows 1 (2, 3, 3, 3, 4) more times: 18 {20, 21, 25, 27, 30} sts at the end of last row.

Row 100 {102, 104, 104, 104, 106}: Ch 1, dc in first st, ✳ ch 1, sk next st, dc in next st; repeat from ✳ across to last 3 sts, dc2tog, dc in last st, turn: 17 {19, 20, 24, 26, 29} sts.

Row 101 {103, 105, 105, 105, 107}: Ch 1, hdc in each st and ch-1 across, turn.

Rows 102 {104, 106, 106, 106, 108}–104 {106, 108, 108, 108, 110}: Work Rows 1–3 of Lace pattern. Fasten off.

FINISHING
Block pieces to schematic measurements. Sew shoulder seams.

Front Edging
With RS facing and larger hook, join yarn in lower front corner, to work up front edge.

Row 1: Ch 1, sc evenly spaced up front edge, across back neck, and down other front edge. Fasten off.

Armhole Edging

With RS facing and larger hook, join yarn at underarm.

Round 1: Ch 1, sc evenly spaced around armhole; join with sl st in first sc. Fasten off.

Darts

Thread a length of yarn, long enough to sew darts closed, onto yarn needle. Working from WS, to finish each dart, flatten the skipped sts of Row 64, so that 1/2 of the sts are on either side of the opening and the sts match. Using locking mattress stitch, **(See page 95)** sew the top edge of the folded section together and into the corresponding sts of Row 65. Repeat on other dart opening. Working from RS, with yarn and using mattress stitch, sew down each pleat, as follows:

First Pleat: Sew together stitches 48 {52, 56, 60, 63, 67} and 81 {85, 89, 93, 96, 100} of Rows 58–65 (these are the sts immediately before and after the skipped sts of the first dart), folding excess fabric into the pleat, so that it lies like the sewn dart row.

Second Pleat: Sew together stitches 113 {125, 136, 149, 159, 172} and 146 {157, 169, 181, 191, 204} of Rows 58–65 (these are the sts immediately before and after the skipped sts of the first dart), folding excess fabric into the pleats, so that it lies like the sewn dart row.

With pleats and darts sewn, the total number of stitches remaining in Row 58 is 129 {145, 161, 177, 190, 207}.

Weave in ends.

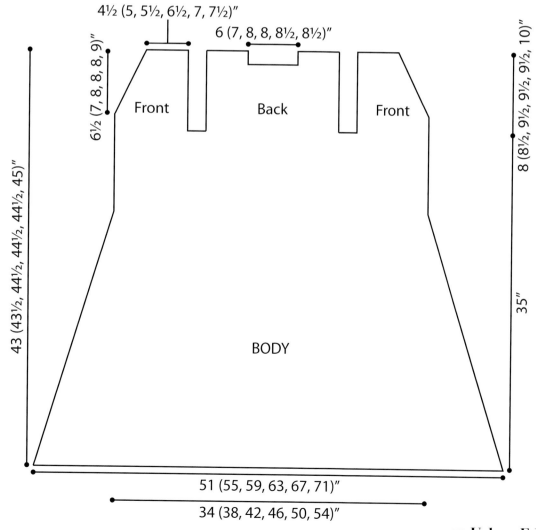

4½ (5, 5½, 6½, 7, 7½)"

6 (7, 8, 8, 8½, 8½)"

6½ (7, 8, 8, 8, 9)"

8 (8½, 9½, 9½, 9½, 10)"

Front

Back

Front

35"

43 (43½, 44½, 44½, 44½, 45)"

BODY

51 (55, 59, 63, 67, 71)"

34 (38, 42, 46, 50, 54)"

Amsterdam

I can't help but draw my design inspirations from the dramatic architecture of the buildings that surround me here in the city. The graphic lines created by the ridges in the fabric of this vest echo those architectural details. Created with my favorite side-to-side construction technique, the Amsterdam Vest is classic enough to wear on a date, contemporary enough to walk the halls of academia and edgy enough to hang out at the skate park.

SKILL LEVEL: ◖■■☐▯ **EASY**

SIZE: Small {Medium, Large, 1X, 2X, 3X}

FINISHED MEASUREMENTS:
To Fit Bust: 34 {38, 42, 46, 50, 54}" / 86.5 {96.5, 106.5, 117, 127, 137} cm, including front borders
Length: 19 {19, 20, 20, 21, 21}" / 48.5 {48.5, 51, 51, 53.5, 53.5} cm

SIZE NOTE:
Instructions are written for Small size with changes for larger sizes in braces { }. Instructions will be easier to read if you circle all the numbers pertaining to your size. If only one number is given it pertains to all sizes.

MATERIALS
Light Weight Yarn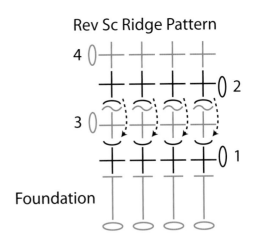
[3.5 ounces, 210 yards (100 grams, 192 meters) per ball]: 3 {3, 3, 4, 4, 4} balls
Shown In: Malabrigo Merino Worsted (100% Merino Wool; 3.5oz/100g, 205yds/190m): Color #9 Polar Morn
Crochet Hook: Size H-8 (5 mm) **or** size needed for Gauge
Yarn Needle

BLOCKED GAUGE: In Rev Sc Ridge Pattern, 14 sts = 4" (10 cm) and 24 rows = 5" (12.5 cm).

GAUGE SWATCH: Block to 8½ x 5" (21.5 x 12.5 cm)
Fhdc 30, turn.

Rows 1–24: Work in Rev Sc Ridge Pattern for a total of 24 rows.
Fasten off.

Rev Sc Ridge Pattern

STITCH GUIDE

Foundation Half Double Crochet (Fhdc):
Ch 2, yo, insert hook in 2nd ch from hook, yo and draw up a loop, yo and draw through 1 loop (first "chain" made), yo and draw through 3 loops on hook (first hdc made), ✳ yo, insert hook under 2 loops of the "chain" just made, yo and draw up a loop, yo and draw through 1 loop ("chain" made), yo and draw through 3 loops on hook (hdc made); repeat from ✳ for desired number of foundation stitches.
(See page 94)

Reverse Single Crochet (Rev Sc): Work single crochet in opposite direction by inserting hook in next stitch (to the right if right-handed, and to the left if left-handed), yo and draw up a loop, yo and draw through both loops on hook.

Rev Sc Ridge Pattern
Row 1 (RS): Ch 1, sc in each st across, DO NOT TURN.

Row 2: Ch 1, working in front loops only, rev sc in each st across, DO NOT TURN.

Row 3: Ch 1, working in free back loops 2 rows below, sc in each st across, turn.

Row 4: Ch 1, sc in each st across, turn.

Repeat last 4 rows for Rev Sc Ridge Pattern.

Notes:
1. Vest is worked in one piece, from side to side.

2. Vest is designed to hang open in front with no closures. Front edges of vest do not meet in front.

Amsterdam Vest ✒

BODY
Fhdc 39, turn.

FIRST FRONT
Note: Piece begins at front edge, increases are worked at the beginning of RS rows to shape front neck.

Row 1 (RS): Ch 5, sc in 2nd ch from hook and in next 3 ch, sc in each Fhdc across, DO NOT TURN: 43 sts.

Row 2: Ch 1, working in front loops only, rev sc in each st across, DO NOT TURN.

Row 3: Ch 5, sc in 2nd ch from hook and in next 3 ch, working in free back loops of Row 1, sc in each st across, turn: 47 sts.

Row 4: Ch 1, sc in each st across, turn.

Row 5: Ch 5, sc in 2nd ch from hook and in next 3 ch, sc in each st across, DO NOT TURN: 51 sts.

Row 6: Ch 1, working in front loops only, rev sc in each st across, DO NOT TURN.

Row 7: Ch 5, sc in 2nd ch from hook and in next 3 ch, working in free back loops 2 rows below, sc in each st across, turn: 55 sts.

Row 8: Ch 1, sc in each st across, turn.

Rows 9–12 (12, 16, 16, 16, 16): Repeat last 4 rows 1 {1, 2, 2, 2, 2} more times: 63 {63, 71, 71, 71, 71} sts.

Sizes S {M, 2X, 3X} Only
Row 13 {13, 17, 17}: Ch 5 {5, 3, 3}, sc in 2nd ch from hook and in next 3 {3, 1, 1} ch, sc in each st across, DO NOT TURN: 67 {67, 73, 73} sts.

Row 14 (14, 18, 18): Ch 1, working in front loops only, rev sc in each st across, DO NOT TURN.

All Sizes

Beginning with Row 3 (3, 1, 1, 3, 3) of pattern, work in Rev Sc Ridge until piece measures about 5 {6, 7, 7, 8, 9}" / 12.5 {15, 18, 18, 20.5, 23} cm from beginning, end with a Row 3 of pattern.

FIRST ARMHOLE

Row 1: Ch 1, sc in first 39 sts, turn; leave remaining sts unworked (for armhole): 39 sts.

Beginning with Row 1 of pattern: Work even in Rev Sc Ridge for 6 {6, 6, 8, 8, 8}" / 15 {15, 15, 20.5, 20.5, 20.5} cm (armhole), end with a Row 4 of pattern.

BACK

Row 1: Ch 29 {29, 33, 33, 35, 35}, sc in 2nd ch from hook and each ch across, sc in each st across, DO NOT TURN: 67 {67, 71, 71, 73, 73} sts.

Beginning with Row 2 of pattern: Work in Rev Sc Ridge until back measures about 11 {13, 15, 15, 17, 19}" / 28 {33, 38, 38, 43, 48.5} cm, end with a Row 4 of pattern.

Second Armhole

Row 1: Ch 1, sk first st, sl st in next 27 {27, 31, 31, 33, 33} sts, ch 1, sc in each remaining st across, DO NOT TURN: 39 sts.

Beginning with Row 2 of pattern: Work even in Rev Sc Ridge for 6 {6, 6, 8, 8, 8}" / 15 {15, 15, 20.5, 20.5, 20.5} cm (armhole), end with a Row 1 of pattern.

Second Front

Row 1: Ch 1, working in front loops only, rev sc in each st across, DO NOT TURN.

Row 2: Ch 29 {29, 33, 33, 35, 35}, sc in 2nd ch from hook and each ch across; working in free back loops 2 rows below, sc in each st across, turn: 67 (67, 71, 71, 73, 73) sts.

Beginning with Row 4 of pattern: Work in Rev Sc Ridge until second front measures same as first front to front neck shaping (about 2 {3, 3 1/2, 3 1/2, 4 1/4, 5 1/4}" / 5 {7.5, 9, 9, 11, 13.5} cm), end with a Row 3 of pattern

Next Row: Ch 1, sc in each st across to last 4 {4, 4, 4, 2, 2} sts, turn; leave last 4 {4, 4, 4, 2, 2} sts unworked: 63 {63, 67, 67, 71, 71} sts.

Next Row: Ch 1, sc in each st across, DO NOT TURN.

Next Row: Ch 1, working in front loops only, rev sc in each st across to last 4 sts, DO NOT TURN; leave last 4 sts unworked: 59 {59, 63, 63, 67, 67} sts.

Next Row: Ch 1, working in free back loops 2 rows below, sc in each st across, turn.

Next Row: Ch 1, sc in each st across to last 4 sts, turn; leave last 4 sts unworked: 55 {55, 59, 59, 63, 63} sts.

Next Row: Ch 1, sc in each st across, DO NOT TURN.

Repeat last 4 rows 2 {2, 2, 2, 3, 3} more times: 39 {39, 43, 43, 39, 39} sts.

Sizes L (1X) Only
Next Row: Ch 1, working in front loops only, rev sc in each st across to last 4 sts, DO NOT TURN; leave last 4 sts unworked: 39 sts.

Next Row: Ch 1, working in free back loops 2 rows below, sc in each st across, turn.

Next Row: Ch 1, sc in each st across.

All Sizes
Fasten off.

FINISHING
Weave in ends. Block piece to schematic measurements. Sew shoulder seams.

Front Border
With RS facing, join yarn with sl st in lower front corner to work up front edge.

Row 1: Ch 1, hdc evenly spaced up front edge, across back neck and down other front edge, turn.

Row 2: Ch 1, hdc in each st across.
Fasten off.

ARMHOLE BORDER
With RS facing, join yarn with sl st in lower, back corner of armhole.

Round 1: Ch 1, hdc evenly spaced around armhole; join with sl st in first hdc.

Sizes 1X {2X, 3X} Only
Round 2: Ch 1, hdc in each st around; join with sl st in first hdc.

All Sizes
Fasten off.

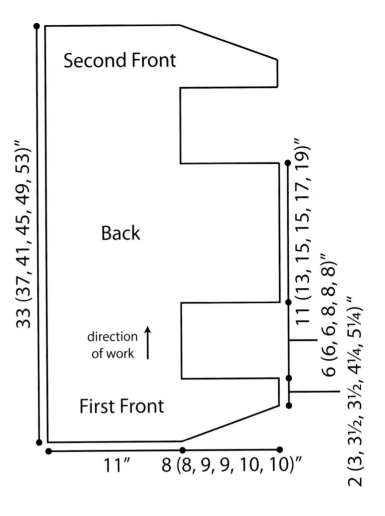

Helsinki

A boyfriend sweater is such a fashion essential that I just had to create one for this book. Using side-to-side construction, I created a sweater with just the right amount of relaxed fit while still conforming to your feminine curves. The bottom ribbing is worked in a pattern that won't bunch up around your hips and the shoulders are set in to the neckline so you have plenty of room to move without feeling confined. The final touch is the oversized cowl neck that is both flattering and adds just the right amount of luxury.

SKILL LEVEL: ■■■▢ **INTERMEDIATE**

SIZE: Small {Medium, Large, 1X, 2X, 3X}

FINISHED MEASUREMENTS:
To Fit Bust: 36 {40, 44, 48, 52, 56}" / 91.5 {101.5, 112, 122, 132, 142} cm
Length: 30 {30, 30$\frac{1}{2}$, 30$\frac{1}{2}$, 31, 31}" / 76 {76, 77.5, 77.5, 78.5, 78.5} cm

SIZE NOTE:
Instructions are written for Small size with changes for larger sizes in braces { }. Instructions will be easier to read if you circle all the numbers pertaining to your size. If only one number is given it pertains to all sizes.

MATERIALS
Light Weight Yarn
[3 ounces, 185 yards (85 grams, 170 meters) per ball]: 9 {10, 11, 12, 14, 14} balls (A), 2 (2, 2, 3, 3, 3) balls (B)
Shown In: Naturally Caron.com COUNTRY (70% Acrylic/30% Rayon from bamboo; 3oz/85g, 185yds/170m): Color #0017 Claret (A); Color #0023 Chocolate Truffle (B)
Crochet Hook: Size F-5 (3.75 mm) **or** size needed for Gauge
Stitch Markers
Yarn Needle

BLOCKED GAUGE:
In ribbing, 16 sts = 3$\frac{1}{2}$" (9 cm) and 21 rows = 5" (12.5 cm);
In main body pattern, 21 sts = 4$\frac{1}{2}$" (11.5 cm) and 16 rows = 4" (10 cm).

GAUGE SWATCH #1: Ribbing – Block to 3$\frac{1}{2}$ x 5" (9 x 12.5 cm)
Note: Ribbing is worked in two colors. Change color at the end of every row.
With A, Fsc 16, turn.
Work in 2-Color Rib for 20 rows.
Fasten off.

GAUGE SWATCH #2: Main body pattern – Block to 9 x 7" (23 x 18 cm)
Fsc 42, turn.
Work in Single-Color Body Pattern for 28 rows.
Fasten off.

STITCH GUIDE

Foundation Single Crochet (Fsc): Ch 2, insert hook in 2nd ch from hook, yo and draw up a loop, yo and draw through 1 loop (first "chain" made), yo and draw through 2 loops on hook (first sc made), ✳ insert hook under 2 loops of the "chain" just made, yo and draw up a loop, yo and draw through 1 loop ("chain" made), yo and draw through 2 loops on hook (sc made); repeat from ✳ for desired number of foundation stitches. *(See page 94)*

Foundation Single Crochet Increase (Fsc-Inc): Insert hook in same st as last st made, yo and draw up a loop, yo and draw through one loop on hook, yo and draw through both loops on hook; to add more stitches follow Fsc instructions beginning at ✳.
Note: This Fsc-Inc is used to add a stitch to the end of a row.

2-Color Rib Pattern
Row 1: With A, ch 1, sc in first st, sc BLO in each st across to last st, sc in last st and change to B, turn.

Row 2: With B, ch 1, sc in first st, sc BLO in each st across to last st, sc in last st and change to A, turn.
Repeat last 2 rows for 2-Color Rib. Fasten off.

Single-Color Body Pattern
Row 1: Ch 1, sc in first st, sc FLO in each st across to last st, sc in last st, turn.
Repeat last row for Single-Color Body Pattern.

Notes
1. Front and back are both worked from side to side.

2. Sleeves are worked from side to side, beginning at the center of one side edge.

3. To change color, work last stitch of old color to last yo. Yo with new color and draw through all loops on hook to complete stitch. Do not fasten off old color. Carry color not in use across top of stitches of previous row and work stitches of new color over the top of the carried strand.

Helsinki Sweater ✒

LOWER RIBBING
With A, Fsc 16, turn.
Work in 2-Color Rib for 151 {168, 185, 202, 218, 235} rows.
Fasten off.

FRONT
Fsc 57 {61, 61, 65, 65, 67}.

SHAPE FIRST RAGLAN ARMHOLE
Row 1 (RS): Ch 1, sc in first st; sc FLO in each st across, Fsc-Inc, Fsc 1, turn: 59 (63, 63, 67, 67, 69} sts.

Row 2: Ch 3 {3, 3, 2, 2, 2}, sc in 2nd ch from hook and in next 1 {1, 1, 0, 0, 0} ch, sc in next st; sc FLO in each st across to last st; sc in last st, turn: 61 {65, 65, 68, 68, 70} sts.

Rows 3–6 {16, 16, 16, 18, 32}: Repeat last 2 rows 2 {7, 7, 7, 8, 15} more times – 69 {93, 93, 89, 92, 115} sts.

Row 7 {17, 17, 17, 19, 33}: Repeat Row 1 – 71 {95, 95, 91, 94, 117} sts.

Row 8 {18, 18, 18, 20, 34}: Ch 4 {3, 3, 3, 3, 3}, sc in 2nd ch from hook and in next 2 {1, 1, 1, 1, 1} ch, sc in next st; sc FLO in each st across to last st; sc in last st, turn: 74 {97, 97, 93, 96, 119} sts.

Repeat last 2 rows 5 {2, 3, 5, 5, 0} time(s): 99 {105, 109, 113, 116, 119} sts.

SHAPE NECK
Row 1: Ch 1, sc in first st, sc FLO in each st across to last st; sc in last st, turn.

Row 2: Ch 1, sc in first st; sc2tog FLO, sc FLO in each st across to last st; sc in last st, turn: 98 {104, 108, 112, 115, 118} sts.

Rows 3–14 {14, 18, 18, 18, 18}: Repeat last 2 rows 6 {6, 8, 8, 8, 8} times: 92 {98, 100, 104, 107, 110} sts.

Rows 15 {15, 19, 19, 19, 19}–22 {22, 22, 22, 26, 26}: Repeat Row 1, 8 {8, 4, 4, 8, 8} times.

Row 23 {23, 23, 23, 27, 27}: Ch 1, sc in first st; sc FLO in each st across to last st; sc in last st, Fsc-Inc, turn: 93 {99, 101, 105, 108, 111} sts.

Row 24 {24, 24, 24, 28, 28}: Repeat Row 1.

Rows 25 {25, 25, 25, 29, 29}–36 {36, 40, 40, 44, 44}: Repeat last 2 rows 6 {6, 8, 8, 8, 8} times: 99 {105, 109, 113, 116, 119} sts.

SHAPE SECOND RAGLAN ARMHOLE

Row 1: Ch 1, sc in first st; sc FLO in each st across to last 3 {2, 2, 2, 2, 2} sts, turn; leave rem sts unworked: 96 {103, 107, 111, 114, 117} sts.

Row 2: Ch 1, sk first st, sl st in next st, ch 1, sc in next st; sc FLO in each st across to last st; sc in last st, turn: 94 {101, 105, 109, 112, 115} sts.

Repeat last 2 rows 5 {2, 3, 5, 5, 0} more times: 69 {93, 93, 89, 92, 115} sts.

Row 13 {7, 9, 13, 13, 3}: Ch 1, sc in first st; sc FLO in each st across to last 2 sts, turn; leave last 2 sts unworked: 67 {91, 91, 87, 90, 113} sts.

Row 14 {8, 10, 14, 14, 4}: Ch 1, sk first st, sl st in next 1 {1, 1, 0, 0, 0} st(s), ch 1, sc in next st; sc FLO in each st across to last st; sc in last st, turn: 65 {89, 89, 86, 89, 112} sts.

Rows 15 {9, 11, 15, 15, 5}–18 {22, 24, 28, 30, 34}: Repeat last 2 rows 2 {7, 7, 7, 8, 15} more times: 57 {61, 61, 65, 65, 67} sts.
Fasten off.

BACK
Fsc 57 {61, 61, 65, 65, 67}.

SHAPE FIRST RAGLAN ARMHOLE
Work same as First Raglan Armhole of Front: 99 {105, 109, 113, 116, 119} sts.

BACK NECK
Rows 1–36 {36, 40, 40, 44, 44}: Ch 1, sc in first st, sc FLO in each st across to last st; sc in last st, turn.

SHAPE SECOND RAGLAN ARMHOLE
Work same as Second Raglan Armhole of Front: 57 {61, 61, 65, 65, 67} sts. Fasten off.

SLEEVE (make 2)
With A, Fsc 5, turn.

SHAPE FIRST SIDE

Row 1 (RS): Ch 3, sc in 2nd ch from hook and in next ch; working in back loops only, sc in next 5 sts, Fsc-Inc, Fsc 4, turn: 12 sts.

Row 2: Ch 6, sc in 2nd ch from hook and in next 4 ch; sc BLO in each st across, Fsc-Inc, Fsc 1, turn: 19 sts.

Row 3: Ch 3, sc in 2nd ch from hook and in next ch; sc BLO in each st across, Fsc-Inc, Fsc 4, turn: 26 sts.

Rows 4–15: Repeat last 2 rows 6 times: 110 sts.

Row 16: Ch 2 {2, 3, 4, 4, 4}, sc in 2nd ch from hook and in next 0 {0, 1, 2, 2, 2} ch; sc BLO in each st across, Fsc-Inc, turn: 112 {112, 113, 114, 114, 114} sts.

Row 17: Ch 2, sc in 2nd ch from hook; sc BLO in each st across to last st, turn: 113 {113, 114, 115, 115, 115} sts.

Repeat last 2 rows 0 {1, 2, 3, 3, 3} more time(s): 113 {116, 122, 130, 130, 130} sts.

Row 18 {20, 22, 24, 24, 24}: Ch 1, sc in first st; sc BLO in each st across, Fsc-Inc, turn: 114 {117, 123, 131, 131, 13} sts.

Row 19 {21, 23, 25, 25, 25}: Ch 2, sc in 2nd ch from hook, sc in next st; sc BLO in each st across, sc in each st across, turn: 115 {118, 124, 132, 132, 132} sts.

Rows 20 {22, 24, 26, 26, 26}–37 {39, 41, 43, 43, 43}: Repeat last 2 rows 9 more times; change to B in last st of last row: 133 {136, 142, 150, 150, 150} sts.

CENTER OF SLEEVE

Row 1 (WS): With B, ch 1, sc in first st; sc BLO in each st across, Fsc-Inc and change to A, turn: 134 {137, 143, 151, 151, 151} sts.

Rows 2–8: Beginning with Row 1 of pattern, work in 2-Color Rib for 7 rows.
Note: You should change to A at the end of Row 8 (Row 7 of the Rib pattern).

Fasten off B. Continue with A only.

Row 9: With A, ch 1, sc in first st; sc BLO in each st across to last 2 sts, sc2tog, turn: 133 {136, 142, 150, 150, 150} sts.

SHAPE SECOND SIDE

Row 1 (RS): Ch 1, sk first st, sc in next st; sc BLO in each st across to last st; sc in last st, turn: 132 {135, 141, 149, 149, 149} sts.

Row 2: Ch 1, sc in next st; sc BLO in each st across to last 2 sts; sc2tog, turn: 131 {134, 140, 148, 148, 148} sts.

Rows 3–20 Repeat last 2 rows 9 more times: 113 {116, 122, 130, 130, 130} sts.

Row 21: Ch 1, sk first st, sc in next st; sc BLO in each st across to last 2 {2, 3, 4, 4, 4} sts, sc in next st, turn; leave rem sts unworked: 111 {114, 119, 126, 126, 126} sts.

Row 22: Ch 1, sc in next st; sc BLO in each st across to last 2 sts, sc2tog, turn: 110 {113, 118, 125, 125, 125} sts.
Repeat last 2 rows 0 {1, 2, 3, 3, 3} more time(s): 110 sts.

Row 23 {25, 27, 29, 29, 29} (RS): Ch 1, sk first st, sl st in next st, ch 1, sc in next st; working in back loops only, sc across to last 6 sts, sc in next st; leave rem sts unworked, turn: 103 sts.

Row 24 {26, 28, 30, 30, 30}: Ch 1, sk first st, sl st in next 4 sts, ch 1, sc in next st ; sc BLO in each st across to last 3 sts, sc in next st, turn; leave rem sts unworked: 96 sts.

Rows 25 {27, 29, 31, 31, 31}–36 {38, 40, 42, 42, 42}: Repeat last 2 rows 6 times: 12 sts.

Row 37 {39, 41, 43, 43, 43}: Repeat Row 23 {25, 27, 29, 29, 29}: 5 sts.
Fasten off.

FINISHING

Block pieces to schematic measurements. Beginning at neckline, sew shoulder and armhole seams. Sew side and sleeve seams. Sew short ends of lower ribbing together, and sew ribbing to lower edge of piece, aligning the seam with one of the side seams.

Oversized Turtleneck

Note: Turtleneck is worked with both A and B; every other stitch is worked with A and every other stitch is worked with B. Carry color not in use across top of stitch of previous round and work stitch of current color over the carried strand.

With Wrong Sides facing, join A with sl st in shoulder seam.

Round 1 (WS): Working around neck edge and spacing the sts evenly, ✳ yo, insert hook in next st and draw up a loop (3 loops on hook), yo with B and draw through all loops on hook (A-colored hdc made), yo with B, insert hook in next st and draw up a loop (3 loops on hook), yo with A and draw through all loops on hook (B-colored hdc made); repeat from ✳ around, ending with a B-colored hdc; do not join, work in continuous spirals.

Rounds 2–23: ✳ With A, hdc in next A-colored st; with B, hdc in next B-colored st; repeat from ✳ around.
Fasten off.
Weave in ends.

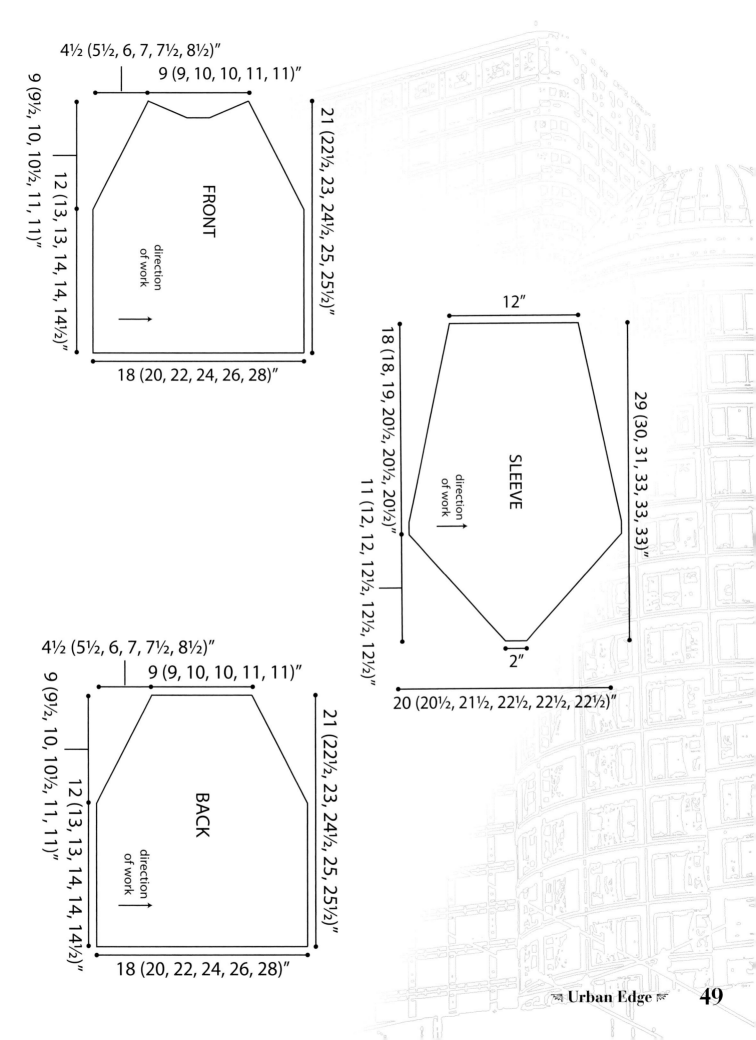

FRONT

4½ (5½, 6, 7, 7½, 8½)"

9 (9, 10, 10, 11, 11)"

9 (9½, 10, 10½, 11, 11)"

12 (13, 13, 14, 14, 14½)"

21 (22½, 23, 24½, 25, 25½)"

direction of work

18 (20, 22, 24, 26, 28)"

BACK

4½ (5½, 6, 7, 7½, 8½)"

9 (9, 10, 10, 11, 11)"

9 (9½, 10, 10½, 11, 11)"

12 (13, 13, 14, 14, 14½)"

21 (22½, 23, 24½, 25, 25½)"

direction of work

18 (20, 22, 24, 26, 28)"

SLEEVE

12"

18 (18, 19, 20½, 20½, 20½)"

11 (12, 12, 12½, 12½, 12½)"

29 (30, 31, 33, 33, 33)"

direction of work

2"

20 (20½, 21½, 22½, 22½, 22½)"

Seattle

With versatility in the front of my mind for the designs in this book, this vest is exactly what I was aiming for. Worn one way, you have a classic drape-front vest with long panels for wrapping in front or tying around your waist. Flip the vest upside down and instantly you have a contemporary twist on a neck wrap that will look FAB as a layering piece. Classic or contemporary... your choice!

SKILL LEVEL: 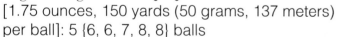 **EASY**

SIZE: Small {Medium, Large, 1X, 2X, 3X}

FINISHED MEASUREMENTS:
To Fit Bust: 34 {38, 42, 46, 50, 54}" / 86.5 {96.5, 106.5, 117, 126, 137} cm
Length: 22 {22½, 23, 23½, 24, 24½}" / 56 {57, 58.5, 59.5, 61, 62} cm

SIZE NOTE:
Instructions are written for Small size with changes for larger sizes in braces { }. Instructions will be easier to read if you circle all the numbers pertaining to your size. If only one number is given it pertains to all sizes.

MATERIALS
Light Weight Yarn 3 (LIGHT)
[1.75 ounces, 150 yards (50 grams, 137 meters) per ball]: 5 {6, 6, 7, 8, 8} balls
Shown In: Malabrigo Silky Merino (50% Silk/50% Merino Wool; 1.75oz/50g, 150yds/137m): Color #415 Matisse Blue
Crochet Hook: Size F-5 (3.75 mm) **or** size needed for Gauge
Yarn Needle

BLOCKED GAUGE:
In pattern, 20 sts = 4" (10 cm) and 21 rows = 5" (12.5 cm).

GAUGE SWATCH: Block to 6 x 5" (15 x 12.5 cm) Fsc 30, turn.

Rows 1–21: Ch 1, sc in first st, sc FLO in each st across to last st, sc in last st, turn.
Fasten off.

STITCH GUIDE

Foundation Single Crochet (Fsc): Ch 2, insert hook in 2nd ch from hook, yo and draw up a loop, yo and draw through 1 loop (first "chain" made), yo and draw through 2 loops on hook (first sc made), ✳ insert hook under 2 loops of the "chain" just made, yo and draw up a loop, yo and draw through 1 loop ("chain" made), yo and draw through 2 loops on hook (sc made); repeat from ✳ for desired number of foundation stitches. *(See page 94)*

Notes:
1. This stitch pattern is reversible and, therefore, should look the same on both sides of the fabric. When instructed to work from RS, select whichever side you like best as the RS.

2. Body is worked in one piece from lower edge up to the underarm. The piece is then divided for armholes, and back and fronts worked separately.

3. When working sc2tog FLO, take care not to work to tightly or the result will be a gap in the work rather than a natural decrease. Make sure the sc2tog FLO looks the same as the Fsc.

Seattle Cross Front Vest ☞

BODY
Fsc 315 {335, 355, 375, 395, 415}, turn.

Row 1: Ch 1, sc in first st, sc FLO in each st across to last st, sc in last st, turn.

Row 2: Ch 1, sc in first st, sc2tog FLO, sc FLO in each st across to last 3 sts, sc2tog FLO, sc in last st, turn: 313 {333, 353, 373, 393, 413} sts.

Rows 3–62: Repeat last row sixty more times: 193 {213, 233, 253, 273, 293} sts.

DIVIDE FOR ARMHOLES
FIRST FRONT
Row 1: Ch 1, sc in first st, sc2tog FLO, sc FLO in next 48 {53, 58, 62, 66, 72} sts, sc2tog FLO, sc in next st, turn; leave rem sts unworked (for armholes, back, and second front): 52 {57, 62, 66, 70, 76} sts.

Row 2: Ch 1, sc in first st, sc FLO in each st across to last 3 sts, sc2tog FLO, sc in last st, turn: 51 {56, 61, 65, 69, 75} sts. Row 3: Ch 1, sc in first st, sc2tog FLO, sc FLO in each st across to last st, sc in last st, turn: 50 {55, 60, 64, 68, 74} sts.

Row 3: Ch 1, sc in first st, sc2tog FLO, sc FLO in each st across to last st, sc in last st, turn: 50 {55, 60, 64, 66, 74} sts.

Row 4: Ch 1, sc in first st, sc2tog FLO, sc FLO across to last 3 sts, sc2tog FLO, sc in last st, turn: 48 {53, 58, 62, 66, 72} sts.

Row 5: Repeat Row 3: 47 {52, 57, 61, 65, 71} sts.

Row 6: Repeat Row 2: 46 {51, 56, 60, 64, 70} sts.

Row 7: Repeat Row 4: 44 {49, 54, 58, 62, 68} sts.

Rows 8–25 {25, 31, 31, 31, 37}: Repeat last 6 rows 3 {3, 4, 4, 4, 5} more times: 20 {25, 22, 26, 30, 28} sts.

Repeat Rows 2–4, 1 {1, 0, 1, 1, 0} more times: 16 {21, 22, 22, 26, 28} sts.

Next Row: Ch 1, sc in first st, sc FLO in each st across to last st, sc in last st, turn.

Repeat last row until armhole measures 7 {7 1/2, 8, 8 1/2, 9, 9 1/2}" / 18 {19, 20.5, 21.5, 23, 24} cm. Fasten off.

BACK
Sk 0 {4, 8, 10, 12, 14} unworked sts following Row 1 of first front, join yarn in next unworked st.

Row 1: Ch 1, sc in same st as join, sc2tog FLO, sc FLO in next 79 {81, 83, 91, 99, 103} sts, sc2tog FLO, sc in next st, turn; leave rem sts unworked (for armhole and second front): 83 {85, 87, 95, 103, 107} sts.

Rows 2 and 3: Ch 1, sc in first st, sc FLO in each st across to last st, sc in last st, turn.

Row 4: Ch 1, sc in first st, sc2tog FLO, sc FLO in each st across to last 3 sts, sc2tog FLO, sc in last st, turn: 81 {83, 85, 93, 101, 105} sts.

Rows 5–28 {28, 31, 34, 34, 37}: Repeat last 3 rows 8 {8, 9, 10, 10, 11} times: 65 {67, 67, 73, 81, 83} sts.

Row 29 {29, 32, 35, 35, 38}: Ch 1, sc in first st, sc FLO in each st across to last st, sc in last st, turn. Repeat last row until back measures same as first front. Fasten off.

SECOND FRONT
Sk 0 {4, 8, 10, 12, 14} unworked sts following Row 1 of back, join yarn in next unworked st.

Row 1: Ch 1, sc in first st, sc2tog FLO, sc FLO in next 48 {53, 58, 62, 66, 72} sts, sc2tog FLO, sc in next st, turn; leave rem sts unworked (for armholes, back, and second front): 52 {57, 62, 66, 70, 76} sts.

Row 2: Ch 1, sc in first st, sc2tog FLO, sc FLO in each st across to last st, sc in last st, turn: 51 {56, 61, 65, 69, 75} sts.

Row 3: Ch 1, sc in first st, sc FLO in each st across to last 3 sts, sc2tog FLO, sc in last st, turn: 50 {55, 60, 64, 68, 74} sts.

Row 4: Ch 1, sc in first st, sc2tog FLO, sc FLO across to last 3 sts, sc2tog FLO, sc in last st, turn: 48 {53, 58, 62, 66, 72} sts.

Row 5: Repeat Row 3: 47 {52, 57, 61, 65, 71} sts.

Row 6: Repeat Row 2: 46 {51, 56, 60, 64, 70} sts.

Row 7: Repeat Row 4: 44 {49, 54, 58, 62, 68} sts.

Rows 8–25 {25, 31, 31, 31, 37}: Repeat last 6 rows 3 {3, 4, 4, 4, 5} times: 20 {25, 22, 26, 30, 28} sts.

Repeat Rows 2–4, 1 {1, 0, 1, 1, 0} more time(s): 16 {21, 22, 22, 26, 28} sts.

Next Row: Ch 1, sc in first st, sc FLO in each st across to last st, sc in last st, turn.

Repeat last row until second front measures same as back. Fasten off.

FINISHING
Front Edging
With RS facing, join yarn with sl st in lower front corner, to work up front edge.

Row 1: Ch 1, split-sc in same sp as join, split-sc evenly spaced up front edge **(See page 93)**, around neck edge, and down other front edge to opposite lower corner, turn.
Fasten off.

Armhole Edging
With RS facing, join yarn with sl st in underarm, to work around armhole.

Round 1: Ch 1, split-sc in same sp as join, split-sc evenly spaced around armhole edge (**See page 93**); join with sl st in first sc. Fasten off.
Weave in ends.

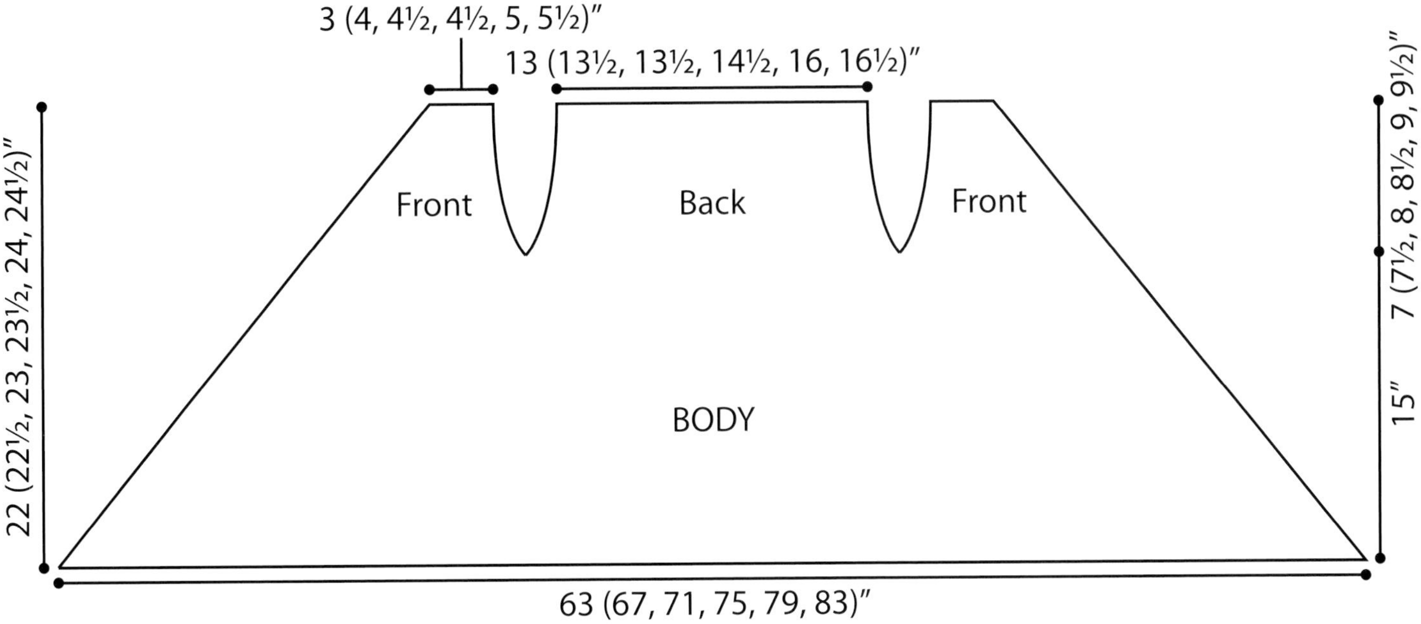

3 (4, 4½, 4½, 5, 5½)"

13 (13½, 13½, 14½, 16, 16½)"

Front

Back

Front

BODY

22 (22½, 23, 23½, 24, 24½)"

7 (7½, 8, 8½, 9, 9½)"

15"

63 (67, 71, 75, 79, 83)"

Bangkok

Every wardrobe needs a "WOW" piece; something with bold lines and sleek design features with just enough edge to set it apart from anything else in your closet. This stand out jacket is that piece. I started with a strong silhouette and stitched the jacket in an exciting fabric that really brings out the asymmetrical lines of the garment. The sharp edges of the collar, layered open front and the wider set of the sleeve caps make this a striking piece to look at and a very special piece to wear.

SKILL LEVEL: ▉▉▉▭ EXPERIENCED

SIZE: Small {Medium, Large, 1X, 2X, 3X}

FINISHED MEASUREMENTS:
To Fit Bust: 34 {39, 41, 46, 49, 54}" / 86.5 {99, 104, 117, 124.5, 137} cm
Length: 27 {27½, 28, 28½, 29, 29½}" / 68.5 {70, 71, 72.5, 73.5, 75} cm

SIZE NOTE:
Instructions are written for Small size with changes for larger sizes in braces { }. Instructions will be easier to read if you circle all the numbers pertaining to your size. If only one number is given it pertains to all sizes.

MATERIALS
Light Weight Yarn
[3 ounces, 185 yards (85 grams, 170 meters) per ball]: 10 {12, 13, 14, 16, 17} balls
Shown In: Naturally Caron.com COUNTRY (25% Merino Wool/75% Microdenier Acrylic; 3oz/85g, 185yds/170m): Color #0012 Foliage
Crochet Hook: size F-5 (3.75 mm) **or** size needed for Gauge
6 Buttons: ¾" / 19mm diameter
Yarn Needle

BLOCKED GAUGE:
In pattern, 16 sts = 4" (10 cm) and 20 rows = 4" (10 cm).

GAUGE SWATCH: Block to 8 ¾" x 8" (22 x 20.5 cm)
Fhdc 35, turn.

Rows 1–5: Ch 1, sc in each st across, turn.

Row 6: Ch 1, sc in first 5 sts, ✻ Spike-Wedge over next 5 sts, sc in next 5 sts; repeat from ✻ across, turn.

Rows 7–11: Ch 1, sc in each st across, turn.

Row 12: Ch 1, Spike-Wedge over first 5 sts, ✻ sc in next 5 sts, Spike-Wedge over next 5 sts; repeat from ✻ across, turn.

Rows 13–36: Repeat Rows 1–12 twice more.

Row 37–40: Ch 1, sc in each st across, turn. Fasten off.

STITCH GUIDE

Foundation Half Double Crochet (Fhdc):

Ch 2, yo, insert hook in 2nd ch from hook, yo and draw up a loop, yo and draw through 1 loop (first "chain" made), yo and draw through 3 loops on hook (first hdc made), ✳ yo, insert hook under 2 loops of the "chain" just made, yo and draw up a loop, yo and draw through 1 loop ("chain" made), yo and draw through 3 loops on hook (hdc made); repeat from ✳ for desired number of foundation stitches.

(See page 94)

Spike: Insert hook into indicated stitch in indicated number of rows below, draw up a loop, yo and draw through 2 loops on hook. Do not work into the corresponding stitch of the current row (it should be covered by the spike stitch).

Spike-Wedge (worked over 5 sts): Spike in next st 2 rows below, Spike in next st 3 rows below, Spike in next st 4 rows below, Spike in next st 5 rows below, Spike in next st 6 rows below.

Spike-Wedge St Pattern (multiple of 10 sts + 5)

Rows 1–5: Ch 1, sc in each st across, turn.

Row 6: Ch 1, sc in first 5 sts, ✳ Spike-Wedge over next 5 sts, sc in next 5 sts; repeat from ✳ across, turn.

Rows 7–11: Ch 1, sc in each st across, turn.

Row 12: Ch 1, Spike-Wedge over first 5 sts, ✳ sc in next 5 sts, Spike-Wedge over next 5 sts; repeat from ✳ across, turn.

Repeat Rows 1–12 for Spike-Wedge St Pattern.

Notes:

1. This stitch pattern is reversible and, therefore, should look the same on both sides of the fabric.

2. Spike stitches are worked into stitches in rows below the row into which you would usually work. The row into which you usually work is 1 row below the working row, the row below the row into which you usually work is 2 rows below the working row, and so on.

3. Body is worked in one piece from lower edge up to the underarm. The piece is then divided for armholes, and back and fronts worked separately.

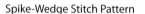
Spike-Wedge Stitch Pattern

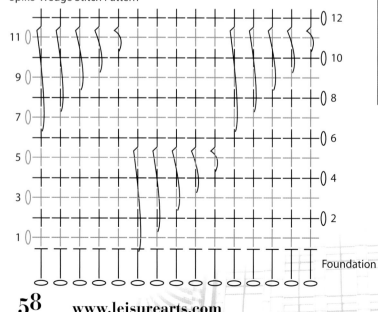

Foundation

Bangkok Jacket ☞

BODY
Fhdc 135 {155, 165, 185, 195, 215}, turn.

Rows 1–50: Beginning with Row 1, work in Spike-Wedge St Pattern for 50 rows.

SHAPE BODY
Row 1: Ch 1, sc in first st, 2 sc in next st, sc in each st across to last 2 sts, 2 sc in next st, sc in last st, turn: 137 {157, 167, 187, 197, 217} sts.

Rows 2 and 3: Ch 1, sc in each st across, turn.

Row 4: Ch 1, sc in first st, 2 sc in next st, sc in next 4 sts, ✳ Spike-Wedge over next 5 sts, sc in next 5 sts; repeat from ✳ to last st, 2 sc in last st, turn: 139 {159, 169, 189, 199, 219} sts.

Rows 5 and 6: Ch 1, sc in each st across, turn.

Row 7: Repeat Row 1: 141 {161, 171, 191, 201, 221} sts.

Rows 8 and 9: Ch 1, sc in each st across, turn.

Row 10: Ch 1, sc in first st, 2 sc in next st, sc in next st ✳ Spike-Wedge over next 5 sts, sc in next 5 sts; repeat from ✳ to last 8 sts, Spike-Wedge over next 5 sts, sc in next st, 2 sc in next st, sc in last st, turn: 143 {163, 173, 193, 203, 223} sts.

Rows 11–15: Repeat Rows 5–9: 145 {165, 175, 195, 205, 225} sts.

Row 16: Ch 1, sc in first st, 2 sc in next st, sc in next 8 sts, ✳ Spike-Wedge over next 5 sts, sc in next 5 sts; repeat from ✳ across to last 5 sts, sc in next 3 sts, 2 sc in next st, sc in last st, turn: 147 {167, 177, 197, 207, 227} sts.

Rows 17–21: Repeat Rows 5–9: 149 {169, 179, 199, 209, 229} sts.

Row 22: Ch 1, sc in first st, 2 sc in next st, sc in next 5 sts, ✳ Spike-Wedge over next 5 sts, sc in next 5 sts; repeat from ✳ across to last 2 sts, 2 sc in next st, sc in last st, turn: 151 {171, 181, 201, 211, 231} sts.

Rows 23–27: Repeat Rows 5–9: 153 {173, 183, 203, 213, 233} sts.

Row 28: Ch 1, sc in first st, 2 sc in next st, sc in next 2 sts, Spike-Wedge over next 5 sts, ✳ sc in next 5 sts, Spike-Wedge over next 5 sts; repeat from ✳ across to last 4 sts, sc in next 2 sts, 2 sc in next st, sc in next st, turn: {155, 175, 185, 205, 215, 235} sts.

Rows 29–33: Repeat Rows 5–9: 157 {177, 187, 207, 217, 237} sts.

Row 34: Ch 1, sc in first st, 2 sc in next st, sc in next 9 sts, ✳ Spike-Wedge over next 5 sts, sc in next 5 sts; repeat from ✳ across to last 6 sts, sc in next 4 sts, 2 sc in next st, sc in last st, turn: 159 {179, 189, 209, 219, 239} sts.

Rows 35–39: Repeat Rows 5–9: 161 {181, 191, 211, 221, 241} sts.

Row 40: Ch 1, sc in first st, 2 sc in next st, sc in next 6 sts, ✳ Spike-Wedge over next 5 sts, sc in next 5 sts; repeat from ✳ across to last 3 sts, sc in next st, 2 sc in next st, sc in last st, turn: 163 {183, 193, 213, 223, 243} sts.

Rows 41–44: Repeat Rows 6 and 7 twice: 167 {187, 197, 217, 227, 247} sts.

Row 45: Ch 1, turn, sc in each st across, turn.

DIVIDE FOR ARMHOLES

Notes: In all remaining sections, you will be instructed to work "as established", this means that you should maintain the Spike-Wedge St Pattern as it has been worked up to this point. There are two important properties of the Spike-Wedge St Pattern that you will need to maintain.

1. The Spike-Wedge St Pattern has a 12-row repeat, consisting of 5 rows worked in sc, 1 row worked in Spike-wedges and sc, 5 more rows worked in sc, and another row worked in Spike-wedges and sc. From here on ensure that this 12-row repeat continues.

2. Each Spike-Wedge row places a Spike-Wedge between the Spike-wedges of the previous Spike-Wedge row, and places sc sts above the Spike-wedges of the previous row.

FIRST FRONT

Row 1: Work in Spike-Wedge St Pattern as established over first 45 {51, 55, 63, 67, 75} sts, sc2tog, sc in next st, turn; leave remaining sts unworked (for armholes, back and 2nd front): 47 {53, 57, 65, 69, 77} sts.

Rows 2–10 {10, 10, 8, 8, 6}: Work even in Spike-Wedge St Pattern as established.

Row 11 {11, 11, 9, 9, 7}: Work in Spike-Wedge St Pattern as established across to 3 sts, sc2tog, sc in last st, turn: 46 {52, 56, 64, 68, 76} sts.

Rows 12 {12, 12, 10, 10, 8}–31 {41, 41, 41, 41, 43}: Repeat last 10 {10, 10, 8, 8, 6} rows 2 {3, 3, 4, 4, 6} more times: 44 {49, 53, 60, 64, 70} sts.

Work even in Spike-Wedge St Pattern as established until front measures 8 {8 1/2, 9, 9 1/2, 10, 10 1/2}" / 20.5 {21.5, 23, 24, 25.5, 26.5} cm from divide. Fasten off, leaving a long tail for sewing.

BACK

Join yarn with sl st in first unworked st following Row 1 of first front.

Row 1: Ch 1, sc in same st as join, sc2tog, continue in Spike-Wedge St Pattern as established over next 65 {73, 75, 79, 81, 85} sts, sc2tog, sc in last st, turn: 69 {77, 79, 83, 85, 89} sts.

Rows 2–10 {10, 10, 8, 8, 6}: Work even in Spike-Wedge St Pattern as established.

Row 11 {11, 11, 9, 9, 7}: Ch 1, sc in first st, sc2tog, continue in Spike-Wedge St Pattern as established across to last 3 sts, sc2tog, sc in last st, turn: 67 {75, 77, 81, 83, 87} sts.

Rows 12 {12, 12, 10, 10, 8}–31 {41, 41, 41, 41, 43}: Repeat last 10 {10, 10, 8, 8, 6} rows 2 {3, 3, 4, 4, 6} more times: 63 {69, 71, 73, 75, 75} sts.

Row 32 {42, 42, 42, 42, 44}: Work even in Spike-Wedge St Pattern as established.

Row 33 {43, 43, 43, 43, 45}: Ch 1, sc in first st, sc2tog, continue in Spike-Wedge St Pattern as established across to last 3 sts, sc2tog, sc in last st, turn: 61 {67, 69, 71, 73, 73} sts.

Work even in Spike-Wedge St Pattern as established until back measures same as first front. Fasten off.

SECOND FRONT

Join yarn with sl st in first unworked st following Row 1 of back.

Row 1: Ch 1, sc in same st as join, sc2tog, continue in Spike-Wedge St Pattern as established to end of row, turn: 47 {53, 57, 65, 69, 77} sts.

Rows 2–10 {10, 10, 8, 8, 6}: Work even in Spike-Wedge St Pattern as established.

Row 11 {11, 11, 9, 9, 7}: Ch 1, sc in first st, sc2tog, continue in Spike-Wedge St Pattern as established to end of row, turn: 46 {52, 56, 64, 68, 76} sts.

Rows 12 {12, 12, 10, 10, 8}–31 {41, 41, 41, 41, 43}: Repeat last 10 {10, 10, 8, 8, 6} rows 2 {3, 3, 4, 4, 6} more times: 44 {49, 53, 60, 64, 70} sts.

Work even in Spike-Wedge St Pattern as established until second front measures same as back. Fasten off, leaving a long tail for sewing.

SLEEVE (make 2)
Fhdc 35 {35, 35, 45, 45, 45}, turn.

Rows 1 and 2: Work Rows 1 and 2 of Spike-Wedge St Pattern for 2 rows.

Row 3: Ch 1, sc in first st, 2 sc in next sc, continue in Spike-Wedge St Pattern as established across to last 2 sts, 2 sc in next st, sc in last st, turn: 37 {37, 37, 47, 47, 47} sts.

Rows 4–8 {7, 7, 8, 7, 7}: Work even in Spike-Wedge St Pattern as established.

Row 9 {8, 8, 9, 8, 8}: Ch 1, sc in first st, 2 sc in next sc, continue in Spike-Wedge St Pattern as established across to last 2 sts, 2 sc in next st, sc in last st, turn: 39 {39, 39, 49, 49, 49} sts.

Rows 10 {9, 9, 10, 9, 9}–87 {83, 93, 93, 88, 98}: Repeat last 6 {5, 5, 6, 5, 5} rows 13 {15, 17, 14, 16, 18} more times: 65 {69, 73, 77, 81, 85} sts.

Work even in Spike-Wedge St Pattern as established until piece measures 18 {18, 19, 19, 20, 20}" / 45.5 {45.5, 48.5, 48.5, 51, 51} cm from beginning.

SHAPE CAP
Row 1: Ch 1, sl st in first 2 sts, ch 1, sc in next st, continue in Spike-Wedge St Pattern as established across to last 2 sts, turn; leave last 2 sts unworked: 61 {65, 69, 73, 77, 81} sts.

Row 2: Work even in Spike-Wedge St Pattern as established.

Rows 3–24 {26, 28, 30, 32, 34}: Repeat last 2 rows 11 {12, 13, 14, 15, 16} times: 17 sts.

Last 2 Rows: Work even in Spike-Wedge St Pattern as established.
Fasten off.

FINISHING
Block pieces to schematic measurements. Sew shoulder seams.

Collar
With WS facing, join yarn with sl st in front top corner, to work across top edge.

Row 1: Ch 1, sc evenly spaced across top of front, across back neck and across top of other front, turn.

Row 2 (RS): Ch 1, sc in first st, working between sps between sts, sc in each sp 2 rows below across to last st, sc in last st, turn.

Row 3: Ch 1, sc in first st and in each st across to end of row, turn.

Row 4 – 9: Repeat last 2 rows 3 times.

Row 10: Repeat Row 2.
Fasten off.

Buttonhole Row
With RS facing, join yarn in top corner of collar, to work across side edge of collar and straigt side edge of top section of right front.
Note: If you are left-handed, join yarn in lower corner of straight, top section of right front, and work across edge to top corner of collar.

Row 1: Ch 1, working in ends of rows across side edge, hdc in first row, * ch 1, sk next row, hdc in next row ; repeat from * to last 2 rows, ch 1, sk next row, hdc in last row, turn.

Row 2: Ch 1, sc in first st, sc in each st and each ch across, turn.

Row 3: Ch 1, sc in first sc, ✳ hdc in next st 2 rows below, sc in next sc; repeat from ✳ to last sc, sc in last sc.
Fasten off.

Front Edging

With RS facing, join yarn with sl st in lower front corner, to work up front edge.

Row 1: Ch 1, sc evenly spaced up front edge, across back neck, and down other front edge, working 3 sc in each corner. Fasten off.

Sleeve Edging

With RS facing, join yarn with sl st at beginning of sleeve cap shaping.

Row 1: Ch 1, sc evenly spaced around sleeve cap, down side of arm, across wrist edge and back up other side of arm. Fasten off. Repeat on 2nd sleeve.

Armhole Edging

With RS facing, join yarn with sl st at underarm.
Round 1: Ch 1, sc evenly spaced around armhole; join with sl st in first sc. Fasten off. Repeat around 2nd armhole.

Sew Sleeves Into Armholes.

Sew sleeve seams.
Attach six ¾" {19mm} buttons to top of left front, opposite buttonholes. Post buttons may be used here.

Post Buttons

To the back of each decorative button, attach a ¼" {6mm} or ½" {13mm} shirt button. Leave a ¼" {6mm} length of thread between the decorative button and the shirt button so this "post" can go through the layers of your fabric. Push the shirt button through the fabric of your garment. This creates a moveable button that can be changed to fit style or color of any garment and can also aid in customizing fit by moving buttons closer to or farther away from the edge of garment.
Note: A set of men's cufflinks can be re-purposed for great post buttons. For added drama decorative buttons can be glued to the top of each.

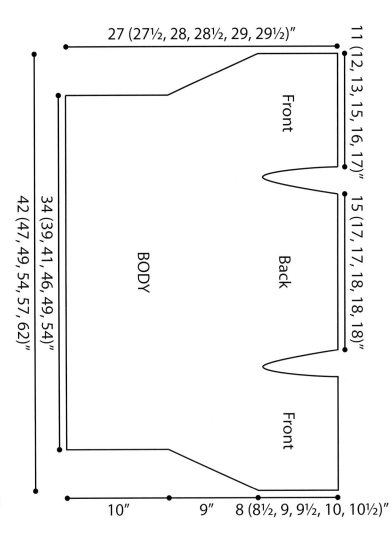

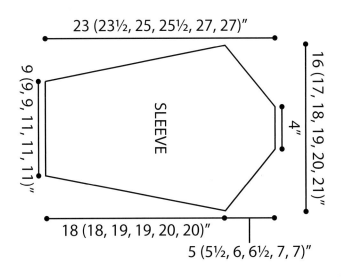

Los Angeles

This piece is another example of real versatility in a garment. I love the fit of a really great long coat that flares a little at the bottom then comes in just the slightest bit for some shaping around the waist. I punched up that classic shape with a very structured stitch pattern to give this jacket visual appeal then finished the front with hook and eye clasps for a very flattering fit. Wear this piece to the office or the theatre then give it a little rock 'n' roll edge by adding the satin ribbons on the sleeves and wear it out on the town to make a real impression.

SKILL LEVEL: ◼◼◼◻ EXPERIENCED

SIZE: Small {Medium, Large, 1X, 2X, 3X}

FINISHED MEASUREMENTS:
To Fit Bust: 34 {38, 42, 46, 50, 54}" / 86.5 {96.5, 106.5, 117, 127, 137} cm
Length: 26½ (27, 27½, 28, 28½, 29}" / 67.5 {68.5, 70, 71, 72.5, 73.5} cm

SIZE NOTE:
Instructions are written for Small size with changes for larger sizes in braces { }. Instructions will be easier to read if you circle all the numbers pertaining to your size. If only one number is given it pertains to all sizes.

MATERIALS
Light Weight Yarn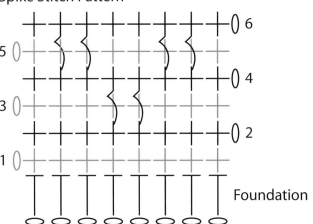
[1.8 ounces, 118 yards (50 grams, 108 meters) per ball]: 21 {24, 27, 30, 33, 36} balls
Shown In: Classic Elite Wool Bam Boo (50% Wool/50% Bamboo; 1.8oz/50g, 118yds/108m): Color #1658 Tomato
Crochet Hook: Size F-5 (3.75 mm) or size needed for Gauge
5 Hook and Eye Closures: TK size
2 3-Yard Lengths of Satin Ribbon
Yarn Needle

BLOCKED Gauge:
In pattern, 16 sts = 4" (10 cm) and 36 rows = 5" (12.5 cm).

GAUGE SWATCH: Block to 6 x 5" (15 x 12.5 cm)
Fhdc 24, turn.

Rows 1–36: Work in Spike St Pattern for 30 rows. Fasten off

Spike Stitch Pattern

STITCH GUIDE

Foundation Half Double Crochet (Fhdc):
Ch 2, yo, insert hook in 2nd ch from hook, yo and draw up a loop, yo and draw through 1 loop (first "chain" made), yo and draw through 3 loops on hook (first hdc made), ✳ yo, insert hook under 2 loops of the "chain" just made, yo and draw up a loop, yo and draw through 1 loop ("chain" made), yo and draw through 3 loops on hook (hdc made); repeat from ✳ for desired number of foundation stitches.
(See page 94)

Spike: Insert hook into indicated stitch 4 rows below and draw up a loop, yo and draw through 2 loops on hook. Do not work into the corresponding stitch of the current row (it should be covered by the spike stitch).

Spike Stitch Pattern (Spike St Pattern)
(multiple of 4 sts)
Rows 1–3: Ch 1, sc in each st across, turn.

Row 4 (RS): Ch 1, sc in first 3 sts, ✳ Spike in next 2 sts 4 rows below (into the Fhdc), sc in next 2 sts; repeat from ✳ across to last st, sc in last st, turn.

Row 5: Ch 1, sc in each st across, turn.

Row 6: Ch 1, sc in first st, ✳ Spike in next 2 sts 4 rows below (into sts of Row 2), sc in next 2 sts; repeat from ✳ across to last 3 sts, Spike in next 2 sts 4 rows below, sc in last st, turn. Repeat Rows 1–6 for Spike St Pattern .

Notes:
1. This stitch pattern is reversible and, therefore, should look the same on both sides of the fabric.
2. Body is worked in one piece from lower edge up to the underarm. The piece is then divided for armholes, and back and fronts worked separately.

Los Angeles Jacket ☞

BODY
Fhdc 148 {164, 180, 196, 212, 228}, turn.

Rows 1–80: Work in Spike St Pattern for 80 rows.

SHAPE BODY
Row 1: Ch 1, sc in first st, sc2tog, sc in each st across to last 3 sts, sc2tog, sc in last st, turn: 146 {162, 178, 194, 210, 226} sts.

Row 2: Ch 1, sc in first 2 sts, ✳ Spike in next 2 sts 4 rows below, sc in next 2 sts; repeat from ✳ across, turn.

Row 3: Ch 1, sc in each st across, turn.

Row 4: Ch 1, sc in first 4 sts, ✳ Spike in next 2 sts 4 rows below, sc in next 2 sts; repeat from ✳ across to last 2 sts, sc in last 2 sts, turn.

Rows 5–7: Repeat Row 3 three times.

Rows 8–12: Repeat Rows 2–6.

Row 13: Repeat Row 1: 144 {160, 176, 192, 208, 224} sts.

Row 14: Ch 1, sc in first st, ✳ Spike in next 2 sts 4 rows below, sc in next 2 sts; repeat from ✳ across to last 3 sts, Spike in next 2 sts 4 rows below, sc in last st, turn.

Rows 15 and 16: Work Rows 3 and 4 of Spike St Pattern .

Rows 17–19: Repeat Row 3 three times.

Rows 20–24: Repeat Rows 14–18.

Row 25: Repeat Row 1: 142 {158, 174, 190, 206, 222} sts.

Row 26: Repeat Row 4.

Row 27: Repeat Row 3.

Row 28: Repeat Row 2.

Rows 29–31: Repeat Row 3 three times.

Rows 32–36: Repeat Rows 26–30.

Row 37: Repeat Row 1: 140 {156, 172, 188, 204, 220} sts.

Rows 38–40: Work Rows 4–6 of Spike St Pattern .

Rows 41–46: Work Rows 1–6 of Spike St Pattern .

Rows 47 and 48: Repeat Row 3 twice.

Row 49: Repeat Row 1: 138 {154, 170, 186, 202, 218} sts.

Rows 50–61: Repeat Rows 2–13: 136 {152, 168, 184, 200, 216} sts.

DIVIDE FOR ARMHOLES

Notes: In all remaining sections, you will be instructed to work "as established", this means that you should maintain the Spike St Pattern as it has been worked up to this point. There are three important properties of the Spike St Pattern that you will need to maintain.

1. The Spike St Pattern has a 6-row repeat, consisting of 3 rows worked in sc, 1 row worked in Spike sts and sc, 1 row worked in sc, and another row worked in Spike sts and sc. From here on ensure that this 6-row repeat continues.

2. Each Spike st row places 2 Spike sts between Spike sts of the previous Spike st row, and places sc sts above the Spike sts of the previous row.

3. Each Spike st row begins and ends with at least one sc.

FIRST FRONT

Row 1: Work in Spike St Pattern as established over first 33 {37, 41, 45, 49, 53} sts, turn; leave rem sts unworked (for armholes, back and 2nd front): 33 {37, 41, 45, 49, 53} sts.

Rows 2–12 {10, 8, 6, 4, 4}: Work even in Spike St Pattern as established.

Row 13 {11, 9, 7, 5, 5}: Work in Spike St Pattern as established across to last st, turn; leave last st unworked: 32 {36, 40, 44, 48, 52} sts.

Rows 14 {12, 10, 8, 6, 6}–37 {41, 41, 43, 41, 49}: Repeat last 12 {10, 8, 6, 4, 4} rows 2 {3, 4, 6, 9, 11} more times: 30 {33, 36, 38, 39, 41} sts.

Next 0 {0, 2, 2, 6, 2} Rows: Work even in Spike St Pattern as established.

SHAPE NECK

Row 1: Ch 1, sc in first st, [sc2tog] twice, continue in Spike St Pattern as established to end of row: 28 {31, 34, 36, 37, 39} sts.

Row 2: Work in Spike St Pattern as established across to last 5 sts, [sc2tog] twice, sc in last st, turn: 26 {29, 32, 34, 35, 37} sts.

Row 3: Ch 1, sc in first st, sc2tog, continue in Spike St Pattern as established to end of row: 25 {28, 31, 33, 34, 36} sts.

Row 4: Work in Spike St Pattern as established across to last 3 sts, sc2tog, sc in last st, turn: 24 {27, 30, 32, 33, 35} sts.

Rows 5–12 {12, 14, 16, 16, 18}: Repeat last 2 rows 4 (4, 5, 6, 6, 7) more times: 16 {19, 20, 20, 21, 21} sts.

Row 13 {13, 15, 17, 17, 19}: Repeat Row 3: 15 {18, 19, 19, 20, 20} sts.
Fasten off.

BACK

Sk 1 {1, 2, 4, 4, 6} unworked st(s) following Row 1 of first front, join yarn with sl st in next st.

Row 1: Ch 1, sc in same st as join, sc2tog, continue in Spike St Pattern as established over next 62 {70, 76, 80, 88, 92} sts, sc2tog, sc in last st, turn: 66 {74, 80, 84, 92, 96} sts.

Rows 2–12 {10, 8, 6, 5, 4}: Work even in Spike St Pattern as established.

Row 13 {11, 9, 7, 6, 5}: Ch 1, sc in first st, sc2tog, continue in Spike St Pattern as established across to last 3 sts, sc2tog, sc in last st, turn: 64 {72, 78, 82, 90, 94} sts.

Rows 14 {12, 10, 8, 7, 6}–37 {41, 41, 43, 51, 49}: Repeat last 12 {10, 8, 6, 5, 4} rows 2 {3, 4, 6, 9, 11} more times: 60 {66, 70, 70, 72, 72} sts.

Next 4 {4, 8, 8, 4, 10} Rows: Work even in Spike St Pattern as established.

SHAPE FIRST SHOULDER

Row 1: Work in Spike St Pattern as established over first 29 {32, 33, 33, 34, 34} sts: 29 {32, 33, 33, 34, 34} sts.

Row 2: Ch 1, sc in first st, [sc2tog] 2 times, continue in Spike St Pattern as established to end of row: 27 {30, 31, 31, 32, 32} sts.

Row 3: Work in Spike St Pattern as established across to last last 3 sts, sc2tog, sc in last st, turn: 26 {29, 30, 30, 31, 31} sts.

Rows 4–9: Repeat last 2 rows 3 more times: 17 {20, 21, 21, 22, 22} sts.

Row 10: Repeat Row 2: 15 {18, 19, 19, 20, 20} sts.
Fasten off.

SHAPE SECOND SHOULDER

Sk 2 {2, 4, 4, 4, 4} unworked sts following Row 1 of first shoulder, join yarn with sl st in next st.

Row 1: Ch 1, sc in same st as join, continue in Spike St Pattern as established to end of row, turn: 29 {32, 33, 33, 34, 34} sts.

Row 2: Work in Spike St Pattern as established across to last 5 sts, [sc2tog] twice, sc in last st, turn: 27 {30, 31, 31, 32, 32} sts.

Row 3: Ch 1, sc in first st, sc2tog, continue in Spike St Pattern as established to end of row: 26 {29, 30, 30, 31, 31} sts.

Rows 4–9: Repeat last 2 rows 3 more times: 17 {20, 21, 21, 22, 22} sts.

Row 10: Repeat Row 2: 15 {18, 19, 19, 20, 20} sts.
Fasten off.

SECOND FRONT

Sk 1 {1, 2, 4, 4, 6} unworked st(s) following Row 1 of back, join yarn with sl st in next st.

Row 1: Ch 1, sc in same st as join, continue in Spike St Pattern as established to end of row, turn: 33 {37, 41, 45, 49, 53} sts.

Rows 2–12 {10, 8, 6, 4, 4}: Work even in Spike St Pattern as established.

Row 13 {11, 9, 7, 5, 5}: Ch 1, sc2tog, continue in Spike St Pattern as established to end of row, turn: 32 {36, 40, 44, 48, 52} sts.

Rows 14 {12, 10, 8, 6, 6}–37 {41, 41, 43, 41, 49}: Repeat last 12 {10, 8, 6, 4, 4} rows 2 {3, 4, 6, 9, 11} more times: 30 {33, 36, 38, 39, 41} sts.

Next 0 {0, 2, 2, 6, 2} Rows: Work even in Spike St Pattern as established.

SHAPE NECK

Row 1: Work in Spike St Pattern as established across to last 5 sts, [sc2tog] twice, sc in last st, turn: 28 {31, 34, 36, 37, 39} sts.

Row 2: Ch 1, sc in first st, [sc2tog] twice, continue in Spike St Pattern as established to end of row: 26 {29, 32, 34, 35, 37} sts.

Row 3: Work in Spike St Pattern as established across to last 3 sts, sc2tog, sc in last st, turn: 25 {28, 31, 33, 34, 36} sts.

Row 4: Ch 1, sc in first st, sc2tog, continue in Spike St Pattern as established to end of row: 24 {27, 30, 32, 33, 35} sts.

Rows 5–12 {12, 14, 16, 16, 18}: Repeat last 2 rows 4 (4, 5, 6, 6, 7) more times: 16 {19, 20, 20, 21, 21} sts.

Row 13 {13, 15, 17, 17, 19}: Repeat Row 3: 15 {18, 19, 19, 20, 20} sts.
Fasten off.

SLEEVE (make 2)
Fhdc 48 {50, 56, 58, 64, 66}, turn.

Rows 1–13: Beginning with Row 1 of pattern, work in Spike St Pattern for 13 rows.

Row 14: Ch 1, sc in first st, 2 sc in next sc, continue in Spike St Pattern as established across to last 2 sts, 2 sc in next st, sc in last st, turn: 50 {52, 58, 60, 66, 68} sts.

Rows 15–27: Work even in Spike St Pattern as established.

Row 28: Ch 1, sc in first st, 2 sc in next sc, continue in Spike St Pattern as established across to last 2 sts, 2 sc in next st, sc in last st, turn: 52 {54, 60, 62, 68, 70} sts.

Rows 29–112: Repeat last 14 rows 6 times: 64 {66, 72, 74, 80, 82} sts.

Work even in Spike St Pattern as established until piece measures 18½ {18½, 19, 19, 19½, 19½}" / 47 {47, 48.5, 48.5, 49.5, 49.5} cm from beginning.

SHAPE CAP

Row 1: Ch 1, sc in first st, sc2tog, continue in Spike St Pattern as established across to last 3 sts, sc2tog, sc in last st, turn: 62 {64, 70, 72, 78, 80} sts.

Row 2: Work even in Spike St Pattern as established.

Rows 3–18 {22, 22, 26, 26, 30}: Repeat last 2 rows 8 {10, 10, 12, 12, 14} times: 46 {44, 50, 48, 54, 52} sts.

Rows 19 {23, 23, 27, 27, 31}–33 {36, 39, 42, 45, 48}: Repeat Row 1, 15 {14, 17, 16, 19, 18} times: 16 sts.
Fasten off.

FINISHING
Block pieces to schematic measurements. Sew shoulder seams. Sew sleeves into armholes. Weave in ends.

Front Closures
Starting at top front of neckline, sew 6 ⅝" hook and eye closures approximately ½" {13 mm} apart.

Sleeve Lacing

- Lay sleeve flat with outside of sleeve facing up and cuff pointing toward you.
- Mark center line of flat sleeve from shoulder seam to cuff.
- Approximately 8" {20.5cm} from cuff, lace ribbon under two sets of spike stitches 2–3" {5-7.5cm} on right hand side of center line then again under two sets of spike stitches 2–3" {5-7.5 cm} to left hand side of center line.
- As if to lace a pair of shoes, and working down towards cuff, cross ribbon and lace through opposite sides of center line stitches. Take care to always lace ribbon under two sets of spike stitches directly beneath the previously laced stitches.
- Continue crossing and lacing just like a pair of shoe laces until you reach the last set of spike stitches at the cuff.
- Repeat for other sleeve.
- Put on garment and tighten sleeves to desired fit by gently pulling laces. Tie at cuff with bow or decorative knot.

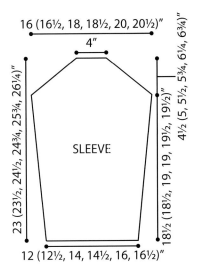

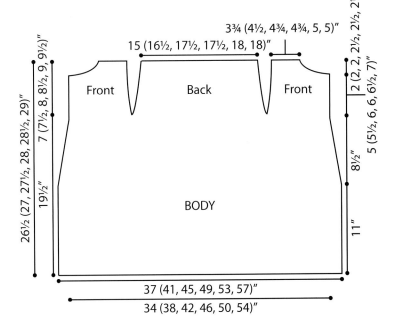

Taos

Being on the front edge of fashion doesn't always mean creating something brand new on the scene. As in the case of the Taos Poncho, edgy can be as simple as tweaking a classic design. I took the shape of the poncho and opened up the top seam with buttons so you can adjust the fit and drape to accompany the whims of your personal style. Simple and classic with a twist... just can't miss!

SKILL LEVEL: ◼◼◻◻ **EASY**

SIZE: One size fits most

FINISHED MEASUREMENTS:
One panel measures about 45" / 114.5 cm long x 17" / 43 cm wide, not including borders

MATERIALS
Medium Weight Yarn
[3.5 ounces, 150 yards (100 grams, 137 meters) per ball**]**: 9 balls (A), 1 ball (B)
Shown In: Malabrigo Twist (100% Baby Merino Wool; 3.5oz/100g, 150yds/137m): Color #862 Piedras (A), #195 Black (B)
Crochet Hook: Size F-5 (3.75 mm) **or** size needed for Gauge
10 Buttons or Toggle Buttons: 1½" / 38mm diameter
Yarn Needle

BLOCKED GAUGE: In Star st pattern, 22 sts = 6 ½" (16.5 cm) and 16 rows = 6 ½" (16.5 cm).

GAUGE SWATCH: Block to 6½ x 6½" (16.5 x 16.5 cm) square
Fsc 22, turn.
Work in Star St Pattern for 16 rows: 11 Stars.
Fasten off.

Star Stitch Pattern

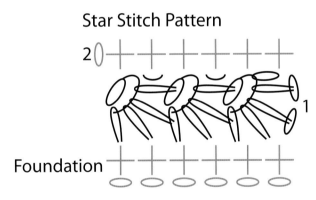

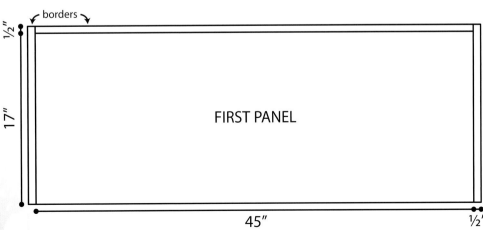

STITCH GUIDE

Foundation Single Crochet (Fsc): Ch 2, insert hook in 2nd ch from hook, yo and draw up a loop, yo and draw through 1 loop (first "chain" made), yo and draw through 2 loops on hook (first sc made), * insert hook under 2 loops of the "chain" just made, yo and draw up a loop, yo and draw through 1 loop ("chain" made), yo and draw through 2 loops on hook (sc made); repeat from * for desired number of foundation stitches. *(See page 94)*

First Star Stitch: Ch 3, insert hook in 2nd ch from hook (skipped ch is arm of first Star), yo and draw up a loop, insert hook in next ch, yo and draw up a loop (3 loops on hook), [insert hook in next sc, yo and draw up a loop] 2 times (5 loops on hook), yo and draw through all 5 loops on hook, ch 1 to close Star and form eye.

Star Stitch (Star St): Insert hook in eye of last Star made, yo and draw up a loop, insert hook into back of 5th loop of last Star made, yo and draw up a loop (3 loops on hook), [insert hook in next st, yo and draw up a loop] 2 times (5 loops on hook), yo and draw through all 5 loops on hook, ch 1 to close Star and form eye of Star.
Note: Loop that is on hook when a Star stitch is started forms the arm of the Star. In Star St Pattern, a stitch is worked into the eye and arm of each star.

Reverse Half Double Crochet (Rev-Hdc): Working in opposite direction (left to right if you are right-handed, right to left if you are left-handed), yo, insert hook in next st to the right (left if you are left-handed) and draw up a loop, yo, draw through all 3 loops on hook.

Star Stitch Pattern (multiple of 2 sts)
Row 1 (RS): First Star, work Star St across, turn.

Row 2: Ch 1, sc in eye of first Star, * sc FLO in next st (arm of Star), sc in eye of next Star; repeat from * across to last st, sc in last st, turn.
Repeat Rows 1 and 2 for Star st pattern.

Note:
To change color, work last stitch of old color to last yo. Yo with new color and draw through all loops on hook. Fasten off old color. Proceed with new color.

Taos Poncho

PANEL (make 2)
With A, Fsc 152, turn.

Row 1 (RS): First Star, work Star St across, turn: 76 Stars.

Row 2: Ch 1, sc in eye of first Star, sc FLO in next st (arm of Star), * sc in eye of next Star, sc FLO in next st; repeat from * across to last st, sc in last st, turn: 152 sc.

Continue in Star St Pattern until piece measures 17" / 43 cm from beginning. Change to B in last st of last row. Do not fasten off.

TOP BORDER
Row 1: With B, ch 1, hdc in first st, 2 hdc in next st, hdc in each st across, turn: 153 sts.

Row 2: Ch 1, sc in each st across, turn.
Fasten off first panel. Do not fasten off second panel.

BUTTONBAND

Note: Work buttonband on second panel only.

Row 1: With B, ch 1, hdc in first st, ✳ ch 1, sk next st, hdc in next st; repeat from ✳ across, turn.

Row 2: Ch 1, sc in first st, ✳ sc in next ch-1 sp, sc in next st; repeat from ✳ across.
Fasten off.

SIDE BORDERS

With RS facing, join A with sl st in corner, to work up side edge of panel.

Row 1: Work Rev-Hdc evenly spaced across side edge to next corner. Fasten off.
Repeat across other side edge of panel. Repeat on other panel.

FINISHING

Block panels to schematic measurements. Beginning at outside ends of top border, place 5 buttons evenly spaced across each end of top border, leaving an 8" / 20.5 cm open for neck. Sew buttons in place. Weave in ends.

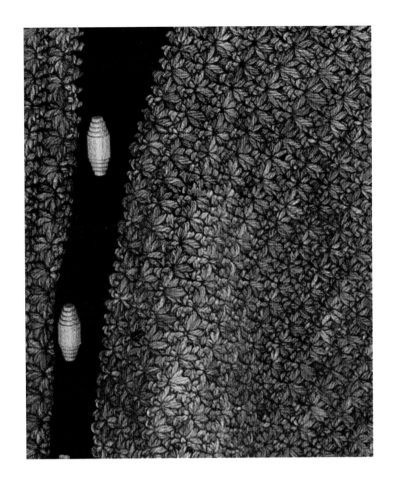

Milan

Often, the city where you work during the day is the same city where you play at night. The challenge has always been to come up with the right wardrobe choices that can make this work to play transition with you. Wear this piece with a jacket and slacks or a skirt and you have the perfect office ensemble with just enough fashion edge. After work, remove the jacket and slip into your favorite jeans or a pair of tights and you quickly transform into that cool woman sipping coffee at the bookstore that everyone wants to get to know.

SKILL LEVEL: ■■□□ **EASY**

SIZE: Small {Medium, Large, 1X, 2X, 3X}

FINISHED MEASUREMENTS:
To Fit Bust: 34 {38, 42, 46, 50, 54}" / 86.5 {96.5, 106.5, 117, 126, 137} cm
Length: 23 {23$\frac{1}{2}$, 23$\frac{1}{2}$, 24, 24, 24}" / 58.5 {59.5, 59.5, 61, 61, 61} cm

SIZE NOTE:
Instructions are written for Small size with changes for larger sizes in braces { }. Instructions will be easier to read if you circle all the numbers pertaining to your size. If only one number is given it pertains to all sizes.

MATERIALS
Light Weight Yarn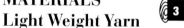
[1.75 ounces, 150 yards (50 grams, 137 meters) per ball]: 6 {7, 7, 8, 9, 9} balls
Shown In: Malabrigo Silky Merino (50% Silk/50% Merino Wool; 1.75oz/50g, 150yds/137m): Color #400 Rupestre
Crochet Hook:, Size F-5 (3.75 mm) **or** size needed for Gauge
Yarn Needle

BLOCKED GAUGE:
In pattern, 25 sts = 4$\frac{3}{4}$" (12 cm) and 25 rows = 7" (18 cm).
Note: Eight (sc, ch 2, sc) pattern repeats measure about 4$\frac{1}{2}$" (11.5 cm).

GAUGE SWATCH: Block to 9$\frac{1}{2}$ x 7" (24 x 18 cm) Fsc 50, turn.

Row 1: Ch 1, sc in first st, sk next st, (sc, ch 2, sc) in next st, ✻ sk next 2 sts, (sc, ch 2, sc) in next st; repeat from ✻ across to last 2 sts, sk next st, sc in last st, turn: 16 ch-2 sps.

Rows 2–25: Ch 1, sc in first st, (sc, ch 2, sc) in each ch-2 sp across, sc in last st, turn.
Fasten off.

Pattern Stitch

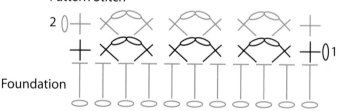

Foundation

STITCH GUIDE
Foundation Single Crochet (Fsc): Ch 2, insert hook in 2nd ch from hook, yo and draw up a loop, yo and draw through 1 loop (first "chain" made), yo and draw through 2 loops on hook (first sc made), ✳ insert hook under 2 loops of the "chain" just made, yo and draw up a loop, yo and draw through 1 loop ("chain" made), yo and draw through 2 loops on hook (sc made); repeat from ✳ for desired number of foundation stitches. *(See page 94)*

Milan Cowl Neck Top ✐

FRONT
Fsc 89 {101, 110, 122, 131, 143}, turn.

Row 1 (RS): Ch 1, sc in first st, sk next st, (sc, ch 2, sc) in next st, ✳sk next 2 sts, (sc, ch 2, sc) in next st; repeat from ✳ across to last 2 sts, sk next st, sc in last st, turn: 29 {33, 36, 40, 43, 47} ch-2 sps.

Row 2: Ch 1, sc in first st, (sc, ch 2, sc) in each ch-2 sp across, sc in last st, turn.

Repeat Row 2 until piece measures 16 {16, 15½, 15½, 15, 14½}" / 40.5 {40.5, 39.5, 39.5, 38, 37} cm from beginning.

SHAPE ARMHOLES
Sizes 1X (2X, 3X) ONLY
Next Row: Ch 1, sl st in first 2 {6, 10} sts, (sl st, ch 1, sc) in next ch-2 sp, (sc, ch 2, sc) in each ch-2 sp across to last 2 {3, 4} ch-2 sps, sc in next ch-2 sp, turn; leave rem ch-2 sp(s) unworked: 38 {39, 41} ch-2 sps.

All Sizes
Row 1: Ch 1, sc in first st, (sc, ch 2, sc) in first ch-2 sp, sc in next ch-2 sp, (sc, ch 2, sc) in each ch-2 sp across to last 2 ch-2 sps, sc in next ch-2 sp, (sc, ch 2, sc) in last ch-2 sp, sc in last st, turn: 27 {31, 34, 36, 37, 39} ch-2 sps.

Row 2: Ch 1, sc in first st, (sc, ch 2, sc) in first ch-2 sp, sc2tog working over next sc and next ch-2 sp, ch 2, sc in same ch-2 sp as last leg of sc2tog just made, (sc, ch 2, sc) in each ch-2 sp across to last 2 ch-2 sps, sc in next ch-2 sp, ch 2, sc2tog working over same ch-2 sp as last sc made and next sc, (sc, ch 2, sc) in last ch-2 sp, sc in last st, turn.

Rows 3 and 4: Ch 1, sc in first st, (sc, ch 2, sc) in each ch-2 sp across, sc in last, turn.

Rows 5–8 {12, 12, 16, 16, 20}: Repeat last 4 rows 1 {2, 2, 3, 3, 4} times: 25 {27, 30, 30, 31, 31} ch-2 sps.

Row 9 {13, 13, 17, 17, 21}: Ch 1, sc in first st, (sc, ch 2, sc) in each ch-2 sp across, sc in last, turn. Repeat last row until armhole measures 4 {4½, 5, 5½, 6, 6½}" / 10 {11.5, 12.5, 14, 15, 16.5} cm.

SHAPE FIRST SHOULDER
Row 1: Ch 1, sc in first st, (sc, ch 2, sc) in each of next 3 {4, 5, 5, 5, 5} ch-2 sps, sc in next ch-2 sp, turn; leave remaining sts unworked for neck and second shoulder: 3 {4, 5, 5, 5, 5} ch-2 sps.

Row 2: Ch 1, sc in first st, (sc, ch 2, sc) in each ch-2 sp across, sc in last st, turn.

Repeat Row 2 until armhole measures 7 {7½, 8, 8½, 9, 9½}" / 18 {19, 20.5, 21.5, 23, 24} cm. Fasten off.

SHAPE SECOND SHOULDER

Sk next 17 {17, 18, 18, 19, 19} unworked ch-2 sps following Row 1 of first shoulder, join yarn with sl st in next ch-2 sp.

Row 1: Ch 1, sc in same ch-2 sp as join, (sc, ch 2, sc) in each ch-2 sp across, sc in last st, turn: 3 {4, 5, 5, 5, 5} ch-2 sps.

Repeat Row 2 until armhole measures 7 {7½, 8, 8½, 9, 9½}" / 18 {19, 20.5, 21.5, 23, 24} cm. Fasten off.

BACK
Work same as front.

FINISHING
Side Edging
With RS facing, join yarn with sl st in lower corner of front, sc evenly spaced up side edge to armhole. Fasten off. Repeat across other side, working from armhole down to lower corner. Repeat side edging on back.
Block pieces to schematic measurements. Sew shoulder seams. Sew side seams.

Armhole Edging
With RS facing, join yarn with sl st in underarm, to work around armhole.

Round 1: Ch 1, sc in same sp as join, sc evenly spaced around armhole edge; join with sl st in first sc. Fasten off.

COWL
With RS facing, join yarn with sl st in shoulder seam at neck.

Round 1: Ch 1, work split-hdc evenly spaced around neck edge, taking care not to tighten or pucker neck opening **(See page 93)**; join with sl st in first st.

Round 2: Ch 1, hdc BLO in same st as join, hdc BLO in each st around; join with sl st in first st.

Repeat Round 2 until cowl measures about 12"/30.5 cm. Fasten off.
Weave in ends.

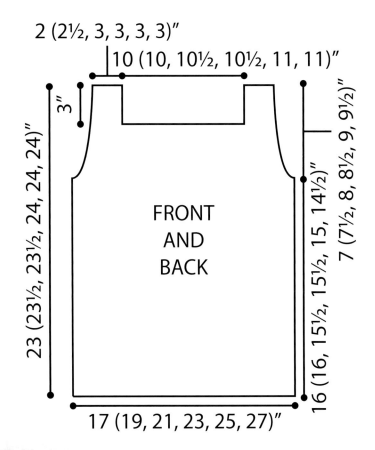

2 (2½, 3, 3, 3, 3)"

10 (10, 10½, 10½, 11, 11)"

3"

23 (23½, 23½, 24, 24, 24)"

FRONT AND BACK

7 (7½, 8, 8½, 9, 9½)"

16 (16, 15½, 15½, 15, 14½)"

17 (19, 21, 23, 25, 27)"

I first envisioned this design years before this book was even a blip on my radar. This piece takes multi-functional design to a new level. No matter what your body type, the simple geometric pattern created by the stitches creates body-flattering lines that will really surprise you. Because of the directional stitches, the resulting fabric has two very different characteristics: one form fitting and another with drape and movement. Express your personal style by wearing the ties around your waist as a skirt or around your neck for a dramatic, stunning dress or cover up.

SKILL LEVEL: ◖■■■□ **INTERMEDIATE**

SIZE: X-Small/Small {Medium/Large, 1X/2X}

FINISHED MEASUREMENTS:
Hip: 36 {44, 53}" / 91.5 {112, 134.5} cm
Length: 31 {31½, 32½}" / 78.5 {80, 82.5} cm, not including tie border

SIZE NOTE:
Instructions are written for Small size with changes for larger sizes in braces { }. Instructions will be easier to read if you circle all the numbers pertaining to your size. If only one number is given it pertains to all sizes.

MATERIALS
Light Weight Yarn (3)
[1.75 ounces, 108 yards (50 grams, 100 meters) per ball]: 11 {14, 17} balls
Shown In: Tahki Cotton Classic (100% Mercerized Cotton; 1.75oz/50g, 108yds/100m): Color #3807 Turquoise
Crochet Hook: Size F-5 (3.75 mm) **or** size needed for Gauge
Stitch Marker
Yarn Needle

BLOCKED GAUGE: In pattern, 16 sts = 4" (10 cm) and 16 rows = 4" (10 cm)

GAUGE SWATCH: Block to 11 x 7" (28 x 18 cm) square

Rows 1–12: Work Rows 1–12 of wrap instructions: 25 sc.

Rows 13–15: Work Rows 106–108 of wrap instructions; 29 sc.

Repeat last 4 rows (beginning with Row 12) 7 times: 71 sc.

Last Row: Repeat Row 12 of wrap instructions: 73 sc.
Fasten off.

STITCH GUIDE

Foundation Single Crochet (Fsc): Ch 2, insert hook in 2nd ch from hook, yo and draw up a loop, yo and draw through 1 loop (first "chain" made), yo and draw through 2 loops on hook (first sc made), ✳ insert hook under 2 loops of the "chain" just made, yo and draw up a loop, yo and draw through 1 loop ("chain" made), yo and draw through 2 loops on hook (sc made); repeat from ✳ for desired number of foundation stitches. *(See page 94)*

Foundation Single Crochet Increase (Fsc-Inc): Insert hook in same st as last st made, yo and draw up a loop, yo and draw through one loop on hook, yo and draw through both loops on hook; to add more stitches follow Fsc instructions beginning at ✳.

Note: This Fsc-Inc is used to add a stitch to the end of a row.

NOTES

1. Wrap is worked as a mitered square, with extra short rows worked from time to time, to form a rectangle.

2. Short rows are worked across only a portion of the stitches in a row. The work is then turned, leaving the remaining stitches unworked. Pay special attention to the turning instructions. Sometimes you will be instructed to turn before reaching the end of a row.

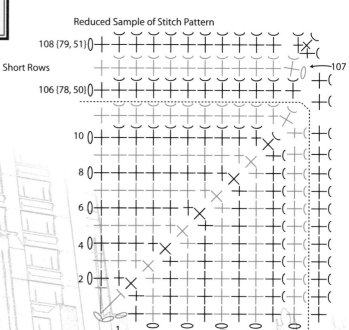

Reduced Sample of Stitch Pattern

108 {79, 51}

Short Rows

← 107 {79, 51}

106 {78, 50}

10

8

6

4

2

1   3   5   7   9   11

Paris Wrap

Row 1: Ch 3, work 2 hdc in 3rd ch from hook, turn: 3 hdc.

Row 2: Ch 1, sc in first st, 3 sc in next st, sc in last st, turn: 5 sc.

Row 3: Ch 1, sc in first 2 sts, 3 sc in next st, sc in last 2 sts, turn: 7 sc.
Place a marker in the center sc of the 3-sc corner at the middle of the row.

Rows 4–10: Ch 1, sc in each st across to marked st, 3 sc in marked st, move marker to center sc of 3-sc just made, sc in each st to end of row, turn: 21 sc.

Rows 11–105 {77, 49}: Ch 1, sc in first st, sc FLO in each st across to marked st, 3 sc in marked st, move marker to center sc of 3-sc just made, sc FLO in each st across to last st, sc in last st, turn: 211 {155, 99} sc.

SHORT ROWS

Row 106 {78, 50}: Ch 1, sc in first st, sc FLO in each st across to marked st, sc in marked st, move marker to sc just made, turn; leave rem sts unworked: 106 {78, 50} sts.

Row 107 {79, 51}: Ch 1, sc in first st, move marker to first st, sc FLO in each st across to last st, sc in last st, turn.

Row 108 {80, 52}: Ch 1, sc in first st, sc FLO in each st across to marked st, 3 sc in marked st, move marker to center sc of 3-sc just made, sc in the end of Row 107 and the end of Row 106, sc in each unworked st of Row 105 across, turn: 215 {159, 103} sts.

Row 109 {81, 53}: Ch 1, sc in first st, sc FLO in each st across to marked st, 3 sc in marked st, move marker to center sc of 3-sc just made, sc FLO in each st across to last st, sc in last st, turn: 217 {161, 105} sts.

Rows 110 {82, 54}–141 {173, 209}: Repeat last 4 rows 8 (23, 39) times: 265 {299, 339} sts.

Rows 142 {174, 210}–144 {176, 212}: Repeat Rows 106 {78, 50}-108 {80, 52}: 269 {303, 343} sts. Fasten off.

FINISHING
Tie Border
Note: *The top of the wrap is the long edge with stitches worked across the edge (not the long edge with ends of rows across).*

Row 1: Fsc 100, working across top edge of wrap, sc in each st across, Fsc-Inc, Fsc 99, turn.

Rows 2 and 3: Ch 1, working in spaces between sts, hdc in each sp across to last st, hdc in last st, turn.

Row 4: Ch 1, working in spaces between sts, sc in each sp across to last st, sc in last st, turn.

Edging Row: Sl st in each st across, do not turn, sl st evenly across side edge of tie, sl st across foundation ch edge of tie to wrap, sl st in edge of wrap. Fasten off.

Edge Other Section of Tie: Join yarn with sl st in edge of wrap where wrap and other section of tie meet, sl st across foundation edge of tie, sl st evenly across side edge of tie; join with sl st in first st of Row 5. Fasten off.
Weave in ends.

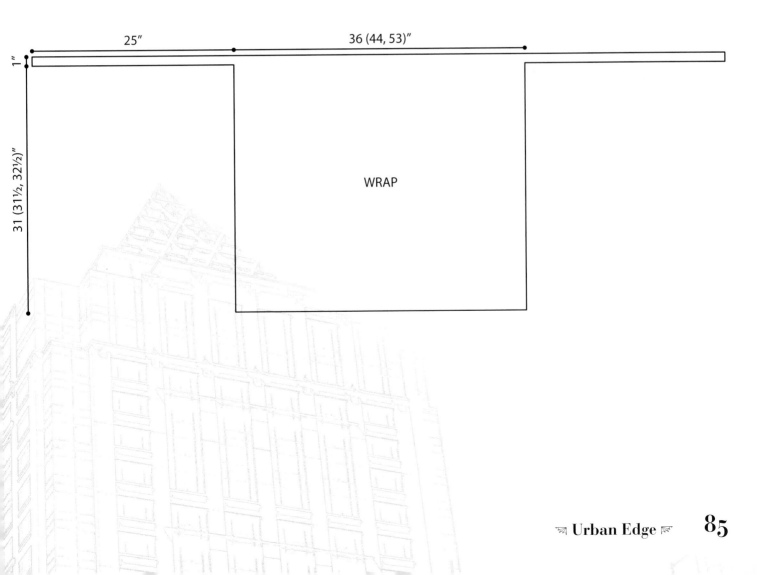

25"   36 (44, 53)"

1"

31 (31½, 32½)"

WRAP

FAB!! That's about all I can say about this dress. I love combining classic crochet techniques with visually stunning, fashion forward designs and this piece just about wraps that up for me. Classic motifs rule the day and give this edgy dress the impact that will make people stop, stare and, yes, be jealous that they didn't make one first.

SKILL LEVEL: ◼◼◻◻ **EASY**

SIZES: Small {Medium, Large, 1X, 2X, 3X}

FINISHED MEASUREMENTS:
To Fit Bust: 32$\frac{1}{2}$ { 35$\frac{3}{4}$, 39, 45$\frac{1}{2}$, 48$\frac{3}{4}$, 52 }" / 82.5 { 91, 99, 115.5, 124, 132 } cm
Length: 29$\frac{1}{2}$" / 75 cm

SIZE NOTE:
Instructions are written for Small size with changes for larger sizes in braces { }. Instructions will be easier to read if you circle all the numbers pertaining to your size. If only one number is given it pertains to all sizes.

MATERIALS
Light Weight Yarn
[3 ounces, 251 yards (85 grams, 230 meters) per ball]: 4 {4, 4, 5, 5, 6} balls of A, 4 {4, 4, 5, 5, 6} balls of B
Shown In: Naturally Caron.com SPA (75% Microdenier Acrylic/25% Rayon from bamboo; 3oz/85g, 251yds/230m): Color #0012 Black (A), Color #0007 Naturally (B)
Crochet Hooks: size D-3 (3.25 mm) (for top and lower borders) size E-4 (3.5 mm) (for motifs), **or** size needed for Gauge.
Stitch Marker
Yarn Needle

BLOCKED GAUGE: One square measures about 3$\frac{1}{4}$" {8.5 cm} across.

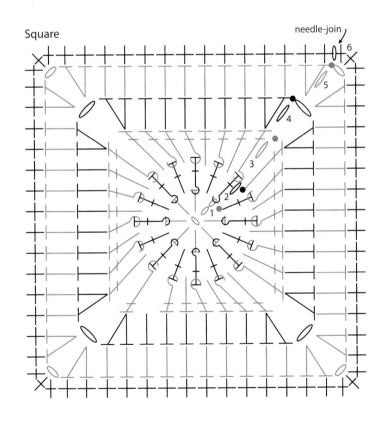

Square

needle-join

STITCH GUIDE

Front-Post Double Crochet (FPdc): Yo, insert hook from front to back and then to front again around post of stitch, yo and draw up loop, [yo and draw through 2 loops on hook] twice.

Notes:
1. Dress is made from square motifs. Each motif is stitched separately.

2. Motifs are arranged as shown in assembly diagram and sewn together. *(See page 90-91)*

3. Top and lower borders are worked after the motifs are assembled.

NYC Dress ☞

SQUARE 1 (make 45 (48, 54, 63, 66, 72)
Center
Round 1 (RS): With A and larger hook, ch 3 (beginning ch counts as hdc), 7 hdc in 3rd ch from hook; join with sl st in top of beginning ch: 8 hdc.

Note: Always work first st of each of the following rounds in same st as join.

Round 2: Ch 1, [FPdc around next st, dc in next sp between sts] 8 times; join with sl st in first FPdc: 16 sts.

Round 3: Ch 1, [FPdc around next st, dc in next sp between sts] 16 times; join with sl st in first FPdc: 32 sts. Fasten off.

OUTER SQUARE
With RS facing and larger hook, join B with sl st in same st as join.

Round 1: Ch 1, 2 hdc in next st, [hdc in next 6 sts, 2 hdc in next st, ch 1, 2 hdc in next st] 3 times, hdc in next 6 sts, 2 hdc in next st, ch 1; join with sl st in first hdc: 40 hdc and 4 ch-1 sps.

Round 2: Ch 1, [hdc in next 10 sts, (2 hdc, ch 1, 2 hdc) in ch-1 sp (corner made)] 4 times; join with sl st in first hdc: 56 hdc and 4 corner ch-1 sps.

Round 3: Ch 1, sc in each hdc around, working 3 sc in each corner ch-1 sp; needle-join as follows: Cut yarn, leaving a long tail. Draw tail up and all the way through last stitch. Thread tail onto yarn needle and insert needle under top 2 loops of second stitch of round. Insert needle back down through center of last st of round and weave under stitches to hide and secure. Duplicate stitch worked.

SQUARE 2 (make 45 (50, 54, 63, 68, 72))
Work same as square 1, working the center with B and the outer square with A.

FINISHING
With WS facing, arrange squares into 9 rows of 10 (11, 12, 14, 15, 16) squares each, as shown in assembly diagram. With yarn needle and yarn, sew squares together using a locking mattress stitch *(See page 95)*. Sew side edges of piece together for back seam, forming a tube (optionally, a zipper can be inserted).

Top Border
Note: Top Border should measure about 2" {5 cm} wide.
With RS facing and smaller hook, join A with sl st in corner of any motif at top of piece.

Round 1: Ch 1, sc in each st around; do not join, work in continuous rounds. Place a stitch marker for beginning of round.

Rounds 2–14: Sc in each st around.

Round 15: Sl st in each st around. Fasten off.

Lower Border

*Note: Lower Border should measure about 1"
{2.5 cm}.*
With RS facing and smaller hook, join A with sl st
in corner of any motif at lower edge of piece.

Round 1: Ch 1, sc in each st around; do not join,
work in continuous rounds. Place a stitch marker
for beginning of round.

Rounds 2–6: Sc in each st around.

Round 7: Sl st in each st around.
Fasten off.

Optional: If desired, a slip with a straight top line
may be sewn into the top border of the dress for
added stability. Use the slip stitch row of the top
border (Round 15) as a guide to hand or machine
sew the matching top border of the slip into the
dress. A shaper-style slip works well for this.

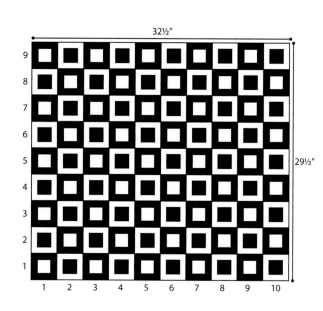

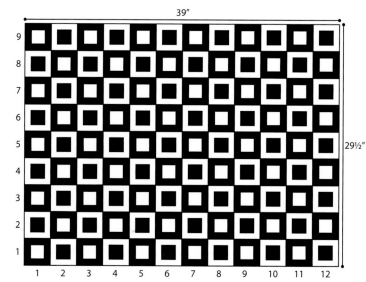

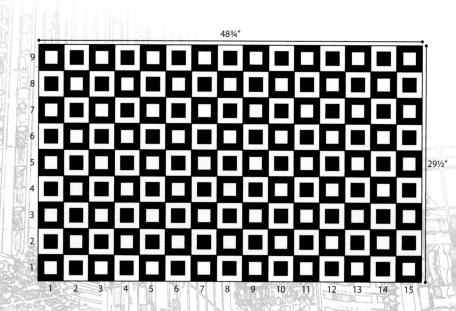

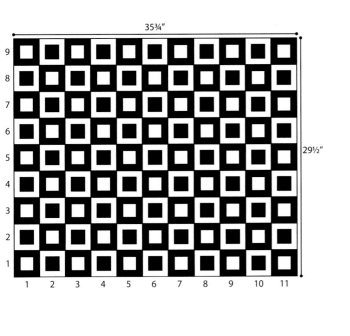

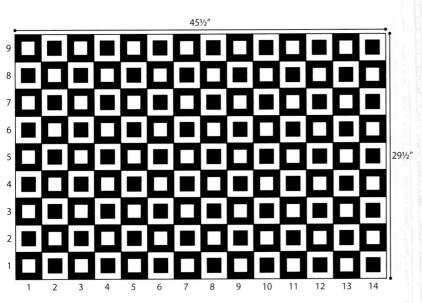

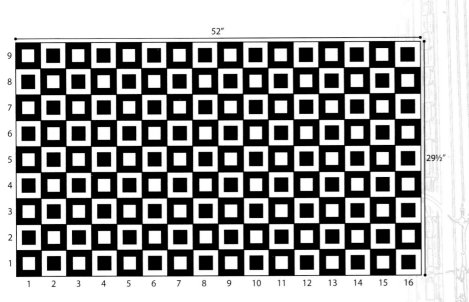

General Instructions

ABBREVIATIONS

BLO	Back loop only
BPdc	Back Post double crochet
ch	Chain
cm	Centimeters
dc	Double crochet
FLO	Front loop only
FPdc	Front post double crochet
Fhdc	Foundation half double crochet
Fsc	Foundation single crochet
hdc	Half double crochet
Ldc	Long double crochet
mm	Millimeters
RS	Right side
Rnd	Round
sc	Single crochet
sl st	Slip stitch
sp	Space
sp-hdc	Split half-double crochet
sp-sc	Split single crochet
st	Stitch
tr	Treble crochet
WS	Wrong side
YO	Yo

( ) or [ ] — work enclosed instructions: As many times as specified by the number immediately following **or** work all enclosed instructions in the stitch or space indicated **or** contains explanatory remarks.

colon (:) — the number(s) given after a colon at the end of a row or round denote(s) the number of stitches or spaces you should have on that row or round.

CROCHET TERMINOLOGY

UNITED STATES		INTERNATIONAL
slip stitch (slip st)	=	single crochet (sc)
single crochet (sc)	=	double crochet (dc)
half double crochet (hdc)	=	half treble crochet (htr)
double crochet (dc)	=	treble crochet(tr)
treble crochet (tr)	=	double treble crochet (dtr)
double treble crochet (dtr)	=	triple treble crochet (ttr)
triple treble crochet (tr tr)	=	quadruple treble crochet (qtr)
skip	=	miss

▬☐☐☐ BEGINNER	Projects for first-time crocheters using basic stitches. Minimal shaping.
▬▬☐☐ EASY	Projects using yarn with basic stitches, repetitive stitch patterns, simple color changes, and simple shaping and finishing.
▬▬▬☐ INTERMEDIATE	Projects using a variety of techniques, such as basic lace patterns or color patterns, mid-level shaping and finishing.
▬▬▬▬ EXPERIENCED	Projects with intricate stitch patterns, techniques and dimension, such as non-repeating patterns, multi-color techniques, fine threads, small hooks, detailed shaping and refined finishing.

Yarn Weight Symbol & Names	LACE 0	SUPER FINE 1	FINE 2	LIGHT 3	MEDIUM 4	BULKY 5	SUPER BULKY 6
Type of Yarns in Category	Fingering, 10-count crochet thread	Sock, Fingering Baby	Sport, Baby	DK, Light Worsted	Worsted, Afghan, Aran	Chunky, Craft, Rug	Bulky, Roving
Crochet Gauge* Ranges in Single Crochet to 4" (10 cm)	32-42 double crochets**	21-32 sts	16-20 sts	12-17 sts	11-14 sts	8-11 sts	5-9 sts
Advised Hook Size Range	Steel*** 6,7,8 Regular hook B-1	B-1 to E-4	E-4 to 7	7 to I-9	I-9 to K-10.5	K-10.5 to M-13	M-13 and larger

*GUIDELINES ONLY: The chart above reflects the most commonly used gauges and hook sizes for specific yarn categories.

** Lace weight yarns are usually crocheted on larger-size hooks to create lacy openwork patterns. Accordingly, a gauge range is difficult to determine. Always follow the gauge stated in your pattern.

*** Steel crochet hooks are sized differently from regular hooks–the higher the number the smaller the hook, which is the reverse of regular hook sizing.

CROCHET HOOKS												
U.S.	B-1	C-2	D-3	E-4	F-5	G-6	H-8	I-9	J-10	K-10½	N	P	Q
Metric - mm	2.25	2.75	3.25	3.5	3.75	4	5	5.5	6	6.5	9	10	15

GAUGE

Exact Gauge is essential for proper fit. All the patterns in this book use a **blocked gauge swatch**. Before beginning your project make the sample swatch(s) listed in the pattern. Then wet block or steam block your swatch to the listed measurements. Count your rows and stitches carefully. If the swatch looks too pulled or you can not block to the correct measurements make another, changing hook sizes to get the correct Gauge. Note that your stitches will not look exactly like the photos until **after** you have blocked the piece.

FRONT LOOP/BACK LOOP ONLY (FLO/BLO)

Work only in loop indicated by arrow. *(Fig. 1)*

Fig. 1

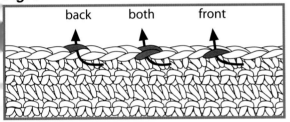

WORKING IN FRONT OF OR AROUND A STITCH

Work in stitch or space indicated, inserting hook in direction of arrow. *(Fig. 2)*

Fig. 2

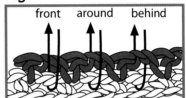

SPLIT SC (split sc)

Insert hook in last stitch worked, yo and draw up a loop *(Fig 3a)*, insert hook in next st, yo and draw up a loop *(Fig. 3b)*, yo and draw through all 3 loops on hook. *(Fig. 3c)*

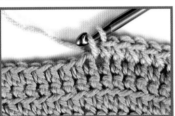
Fig. 3a

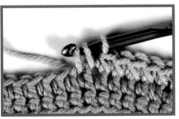
Fig. 3b

Fig. 3c

SPLIT HALF-DOUBLE CROCHET (split hdc)

Yo, insert hook in last st worked, yo and draw up a loop *(Fig. 4a)*, insert hook in next st, yo and draw up a loop *(Fig. 4b)*, yo and draw through all 4 loops on hook. *(Fig. 4c)*

Fig. 4a

Fig. 4b

Fig. 4c

Why use the "Foundation" stitches rather than traditional chain stitches?
The *Foundation Single Crochet* and *Foundation Half Double Crochet* provide a bottom hem that has more stretch than a standard chain. This is needed for many of the designs in this book. They also add a polished look and are better for working back into for borders as well as adding length.

FOUNDATION SINGLE CROCHET (Fsc):

Ch 2, insert hook in 2nd ch from hook, yo and draw up a loop *(Fig. 5a)*, yo and draw through 1 loop (first "chain" made) *(Fig 5b)*, yo and draw through 2 loops on hook (first sc made) *(Fig. 5C)*, ✳ insert hook under 2 loops of the "chain" just made, yo and draw up a loop, yo and draw through 1 loop ("chain" made), yo and draw through 2 loops on hook (sc made); repeat from ✳ for desired number of foundation stitches. *(Fig. 5d)*.

FOUNDATION HALF-DOUBLE CROCHET

(Fhdc): Ch 2, yo, insert hook in 2nd ch from hook, yo and draw up a loop *(Fig. 6a)*, yo and draw through 1 loop (first "chain" made) *(Fig. 6b)*, yo and draw through 3 loops on hook (first hdc made) *(Fig. 6c)*, ✳ yo, insert hook under 2 loops of the "chain" just made, yo and draw up a loop, yo and draw through 1 loop ("chain" made), yo and draw through 3 loops on hook (hdc made); repeat from ✳ for desired number of foundation stitches. *(Fig. 6d)*.

Fig. 5a

Fig. 5b

Fig. 6a

Fig. 6b

Fig. 5c

Fig. 5d

Fig. 6c

Fig. 6d

SEWING WITH A LOCKING MATTRESS STITCH

The Locking Mattress Stitch differs from the standard Mattress Stitch in that, rather than moving directly up the seam to the next stitch on each side, you return back to the preceeding stitch before advancing. This locks in the stitch creating a strong seam that is invisible from the right side.

Directions:

- Lay work with RS down and edges to be sewn side by side. Stitches will be worked through the top loop only of both sides.
- Insert needle from left to right through the first stitches of both panels at the bottom of your work to begin joining the two panels.
- Now insert needle from right to left into the next stitch of the right panel and continue through the last stitch worked on the left panel. *(Fig. 7a)*
- Next, insert needle from left to right into the next stitch of the left panel and continue through the last stitch worked of the right panel. *(Fig. 7b)*
- Continue in this manner gently pulling the yarn snug as you go to close the seam. *(Fig. 7c)*
- Every few stitches pull the yarn tight to secure and even out the seam. *(Fig. 7d)*
- Weave in ends.

Fig. 7a

Fig. 7b

Fig. 7c

Fig. 7d

SYMBOL KEY

◯ = chain (ch)

● = slip stitch (sl st)

+ = single crochet (sc)

≈ = reverse single crochet (rev sc)

⊤ = half double crochet (hdc)

† = double crochet (dc)

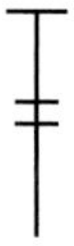

‡ = treble crochet (tr)

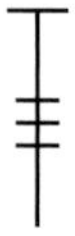

‡ = double treble crochet (dtr)

= Front Post double crochet (FPdc)

= Front Post treble crochet (FPtr)

= Front Post double treble crochet (FPdtr)

‿ = in front loop only (FLO)

⌢ = in back loop only (BLO)

= spike SC

= Star stitch

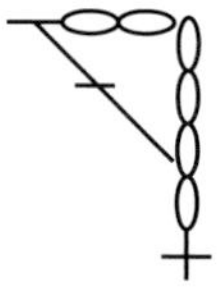

= beginning Y-stitch (beg Y-st)

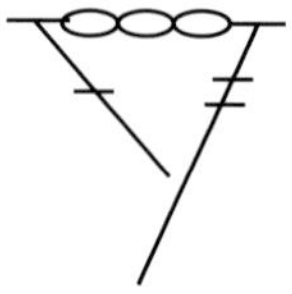

= Y-stitch (Y-st)

= ending Y-stitch (end Y-st)

= FPdc-Cross st

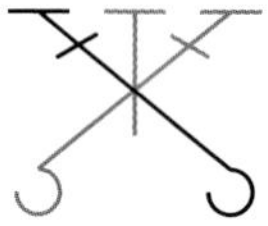

= 1-over-1 FPdc-Cable

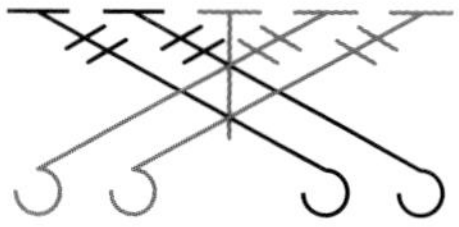

= 2-over-2 FPtr-Cable

= 1-over-1 FPtr-Cable

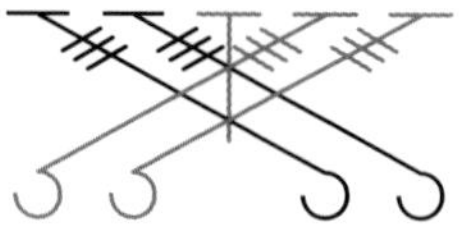

= 2-over-2 FPdtr-Cable

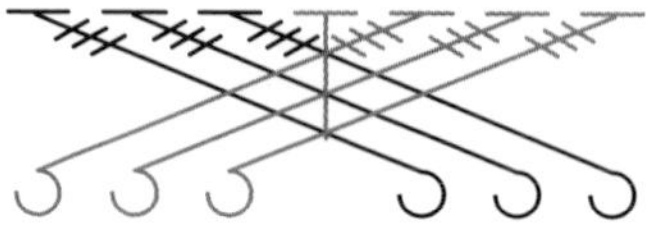

= 3-over-3 FPdtr-Cable